AN ESSAY ON THE ORIGIN OF THE SOUTH INDIAN TEMPLE

AN
ESSAY ON THE ORIGIN
OF THE
SOUTH INDIAN TEMPLE

N. VENKATA RAMANAYYA

GYAN

Published by

GYAN

Gyan Publishing House
5, Ansari Road
Daryaganj, New Delhi-110002
Phone: 011-47034999, 9811692060
E-mail: books@gyanbooks.com

Distribution Network
gyanbooks.com
India, USA, Canada, UK, Australia, France

ISBN : 978-81-212-3353-8 (PB)
First Published, 1930

2nd Impression 2020

Printed at: Gyan Press, Delhi.

AnEssay on the Origin of the South Indian Temple
Author: N. Venkata Ramanayya

An Essay

ON THE

Origin of the South Indian Temple

BY

N. VENKATA RAMANAYYA, M. A., Ph. D.
Madras Christian College

DOCTRINA-VIM-PROMOVET INSITAM

THE TABLE OF CONTENTS

PREFACE

A thesis for a doctorate in Philosophy must, according to the regulations of the University, either embody new facts brought to light by the candidate, or contain original deductions based upon already known facts. It is difficult to assign the following either to the one or the other of these classes; for it contains a few facts which have been observed by me. However, it may be assigned to the second class, as it is mainly based on facts collected by others. I am also required to say how far the essay is original. I do not claim originality for most of the facts mentioned in the essay. I have duly acknowledged my indebtedness to various authors from whom I collected them. I happened to gather a number of facts on the subject, while conducting an investigation into the origin of the Linga cult. A hypothesis had gradually taken shape in my mind, unconsciously, as it were. A study of the theory of the origin of the Dravidian temple propounded by Mr. Longhurst (Arch. Rep. 1915-16) showed me the way in which I should conduct the enquiry. The work of tracing the evolution of the South Indian Temple step by step is entirely mine. Although I at first accepted the current theories regarding the origin of the Hindu Temple and the South Indian Vimanas, I was soon convinced that in the light of facts that came under my purview they were untenable. I had, therefore, to go deeper into the matter than I at first wanted. I have attempted to show in the course of my essay that the Hindu Temple was not modelled upon the Buddhist Stupa, but that it existed anterior to the Stupa. In fact, it served as a model to the early low domical stupa which in course of ages assumed the shape of a tower, resembling a temple Vimana. I have endeavoured to show that the South Indian Temple acquired its Vimana, as a result of a number of causes which brought the temple and the Vimana together. All these are the results of my own thinking; and so far as I am aware, I am not indebted to any one in this respect. I must express my gratitude to the late Mr. A. Mahadeva Sastri, the Curator, the Adyar Theosophical Library for his valuable assistance in lending me books, and suggesting to me fresh sources of information, and to my brother Mr. N. Raghavayya, M.A. for his valuable suggestions and criticisms. I take this opportunity to thank my esteemed friend Mr. K. Narasimhachari who, in spite of his multifarious activities, supplied me with all the diagrams that I wanted for the purposes of this essay. I owe a debt of thanks to my friend Mr. D. T. Subrahmanian, B.A. (Hon.), Lecturer, Islamia College, Vaniyambadi for compiling the index.

PURASWAKAM,
March 21, 1930.

N. V. R.

LIST OF ILLUSTRATIONS

CHAPTER 1

INTRODUCTORY

The term 'The Dravidian Temple' is often met with in the histories of Indian Art. It is applied to our temple in order to distinguish it from that of Northern India and Deccan. The need for such a distinction is obvious. Our temples differ from those of the north in certain important respects; and it is not reasonable to include both of them in the same class. However, when once this distinction is made, it gives rise to certain new problems which demand solution. The most important of them is the one concerning the origin of the difference between the temples of the north and the south. What are the causes that have given birth to this difference? In other words, what is the origin of the Dravidian or South Indian temple? The question is more easily asked than answered. Answers more or less satisfactory have been given from time to time. However, it cannot be said that the problem has been completely solved. It is too complex to admit of a simple solution. An attempt is made in the following pages to study the problem from a new standpoint.

It is generally supposed that there is a single type of temple in South India called the Dravidian temple. This is a mistake. There are, in fact, two kinds of temples which are generally seen all over Southern India : the temples dedicated to the higher gods of the Hindu pantheon, and those built in honour of the village deities. The latter again fall into two classes : some are built in the shape of a dolmen, whereas the others are modelled upon the hut-urn. In addition to these, we have to consider the temples that are peculiar to certain localities. Although the teriari and the boath are seen nowhere else except among the Todas of the Nilgiris they seem to have exercised as much influence upon the Dravidian temple as the Suḍalai-Mâḍan shrines of Tinnevelly. The present South Indian temple is the result of a syncretism of all these.

We have also to notice another important point in this connection. All the temples that have been mentioned above are intimately connected with the grave-yard or the cremation ground.

The connection with the graves is seen not only in the case of the temples of the village deities, but in that of the temples of certain gods like Śiva, belonging to a higher plane of divine life. The earliest reference to Śiva's association with the cremation ground comes from the *Mahābhārata*. In ch. 141 of the Anuśāsana-parvan, the god himself declares that there is no spot 'that is more sacred than the śmaśāna.' Therefore, he adds, 'The crematorium of all places pleases my heart..... Hence the crematorium is the sacred abode to me; ... it seems to me to be the very heaven.'[1]

The author of this episode seems to be alluding to the temples of Śiva built in the crematories. Whether he does so or not, is not of very great consequence; but the passage establishes a very early connection of Śiva with the cremation ground. Moreover, it also gives us a reason why the temples of Śiva, in almost all the important places of pilgrimage stand, or have at one time stood, in the cremation ground itself. It is probably for this reason that some of our ancient *śilpa-śāstras* enjoin that the temples of Śiva should be built outside the precincts of villages.[2] Moreover, there is ample epigraphical evidence to show that, in certain cases, temples of Śiva were actually built upon graves. Mr. H. Krishna Śāstri informs us that "there is a record of the 9th century A.D., at Sōḷapuram in North Arcot district, recording that the Chôḷa king Rājâditya caused to be built a temple to Īśvara (Śiva) on the spot where his father had been buried." "Another inscription records that at Toṇḍamanāḍ in Chittoor district was built a shrine over or near the burial ground (*paḻḻip-paḍai*) of the Chôḷa king Âditya I. A third inscription found in the Chôḷêśvara temple at Mêlpâḍi states that Rājarāja I at the end of the 10th century A.D., had been pleased to build the temple of Ariñjîśvara as a *paḻḻippaḍai* for the lord who died at Aṟṟûr."[3]

The numerous temples that are dedicated to the god Śmaśânêśvara in many places in South India might have had a similar origin. They generally stand in or near the grave-yards. The custom of building Śiva's temples over graves is by no means dead. Many communities in South India, such as the Lingāyats, Kammālans, Jānḍras, Veḷḷālars, &c., still observe it; but a temple is not built in every case of burial or cremation, because the poor cannot afford it. However, they set up a *lingam* over the graves. The rich still build miniature Śiva

A temple of the village deity.

shrines over them. It is not at all an uncommon sight for a casual visitor to a South Indian Hindu grave-yard, to see a small shrine containing a *lingam* raising its head over hundreds of *lingas* set up on the graves in the neighbourhood.

The connection of the temple with the grave-yard, therefore, appears to be intimate and ancient. The temple of Śiva seems to be closely connected with those of the village deities. An attempt is here made to examine the nature of this relationship, in order to discover the lines on which the modern South Indian temple has been evolved.

References :—

[1] *Mahabharata.* P. C. Roy's English Translation.

[2] Ram Raz's *Essay on Indian Architecture.*

[3] Report of Arch. Sur., Southern Circle, 1915-16.

CHAPTER II

THE SACRED TREE

The South Indian temple had, at the beginning, no connection with the worship of any deity. The various gods and goddesses whom the indigenous population of the peninsula worshipped were not accustomed to dwell in the secluded atmosphere of the temples; they loved the life in the open air. This becomes very clear when we take into consideration the cults of some of the primitive deities who have not yet lost their primitive character. They are very popular, and their influence over the lives of people is very great. The typical deity of the South Indian village is the *grâmadêvatā* or the village deity, who is generally lodged in a small shrine constructed on a primitive pattern. The shrine, however, marks a late stage in the development of the cult of the *grâmadêvatā*. It is still possible for us to discern an earlier stage of the cult. In a large number of villages, the *grâmadêvatās* have no temples at all; they are lodged in the open air in the shadow of a big tree. In a good number of villages, no object is placed to represent the deity. In all these places, the tree itself is regarded as the embodiment of the deity. This is the sacred tree of the village; and it receives all acts of worship which are meant for the deity. The tree which is usually considered sacred to the *grâmadêvatā* is the margosa. This, however, is not always the case. Sometimes, the goddess takes a fancy for some other kind of tree or group of trees. Munīśvara, a malevolent spirit, belonging to the class of village gods, lives under any tree. He is not very particular in the choice of his sacred tree. He may live under a huge banyan as he does near the Eḷāvūr Railway Station; or he may take a special liking to mango trees as he does in some of the villages in the vicinity of Kāḷahasti.

Next in importance to the *grâmadêvatā* and more popular is Vināyaka. He has his own temples in the Tamil country; but an independent temple of this god is seldom seen in the Ândhradêśa. Here, he usually lives in the open country, in the midst of paddy fields, on the banks of water channels. He usually takes his seat under some tree, even though it be a solitary palmyra. Occasionally, he is also seen standing in the midst of fields without any covering over his head.

The love of the open air is not a peculiar feature of these minor gods. Some of the great gods of the Hindu pantheon exhibit traces of a forgotten past, when they seem to have lived under trees. Both Śiva and Vishṇu the most important gods whom the Hindus worship at the present day, appear to have had no temples in the distant past. The *linga,* the universal emblem of Śiva is seen not only in temples, but in the midst of dense forests, with no covering over its head except the branches of the sacred *bilva* tree. The holy *aśvattha* is as closely associated with Vishṇu as the *bilva* with Śiva. It is generally believed that the god lives within the tree. These instances are enough to show that the gods of South India had no temples at the beginning. Almost all of them were worshipped in the form of trees. This simple form of primitive worship still survives, although the people have learnt to build very beautiful houses for their gods to live in.

CHAPTER III

THE PRE-HISTORIC GRAVES

From what has been said in the previous chapter, it must have become clear that the origin of our temple cannot be traced to the cult of any god. It had its birth in certain social and quasi-religious practices, which had no connection whatever with the worship of any particular god or goddess. We must look for its origin in the innumerable pre-historic graves that are seen everywhere in certain parts of South India and the Deccan. The credit of having indicated this line of investigation must go to Mr. Longhurst, the present Superintendent of Archæology, Southern Circle. Although his exposition of the subject is brilliant, his conclusions are not very convincing. This is, perhaps, due to the fact that he confines his attention too exclusively to archæological finds. It is necessary to consider the problem from two or three different stand-points, in order to achieve more satisfactory results.

"It is clear," he observes, "that in ancient India, ancestor-worship, or more broadly the cult of the dead, formed the staple of religious belief of the original inhabitants in early times." [1] This statement is not quite accurate. It must be noted, in the first place, that ancestor-worship strictly speaking, did not form 'the staple of religious belief of the original inhabitants.' A study of the religion of some of the South Indian tribes, whose beliefs are supposed to have suffered no change, clearly shows that they worship gods other than the spirits of the departed ancestors. The gods occupy a more important place in the minds of these savages than the ancestor-spirits. Secondly, it is not very clear what Mr. Longhurst really means, when he speaks of 'ancestor-worship or more broadly the cult of the dead.' The worship of the spirits of the departed was reduced into a system by the Indo-Aryans. Such a system was not known to the non-Aryan communities. It must be admitted, however, that certain distinguished men received divine honours in every tribe; but this is not ancestral worship. The 'cult of the manes' can only grow when a community develops a fairly high degree of historical sense. Until a community learns to link the past

Sudalai Madan Pillar.

with the present, it is not possible for it to conceive of a state of society where spirits of the departed ancestors of several generations are expected to exercise some influence. Neither finds in the pre-historic graves, nor the religious observances of the primitive tribes inhabiting the country justify the conclusion that the worship of ancestral spirits was known to the non-Aryans. It is true that there was a 'cult of the dead.' Mr. Longhurst does not tell us what exactly its nature was. His meaning is not clear; and the co-ordination of the phrases—'ancestor-worship' and 'the cult of the dead' is certainly misleading. It is necessary that we should determine the nature of 'the cult of the dead' which flourished in South India. This cult did not involve the worship of the spirits of all the dead persons. Only the spirits of those who had won great notoriety during their earthly career received worship. Among the Gollas, Îḍigas, Byaḍaru, etc., the common belief is that good men after their death become *vîrulu*, 'heroes,' and they are worshipped at regular intervals. The spirits of the wicked are feared. They are supposed to cause epidemics and famines. Unless their anger is appeased, they continue their work of destruction. Year after year new temples are built in honour of the spirits of the wicked persons and of those that suffered violent death. The temples of Kanakadurgamma, Podilamma, Thôṭakūramma, Kôṭappakoṇḍa svâmi, and a host of local deities all over the Telugu districts had their origin in this fashion. Now the worship of all these goddesses and gods is certainly a 'cult of the dead.' But it is neither 'ancestor-worship' nor the worship of the spirits of all the dead persons. It is the worship of the dead notables. It is to 'the cult of the dead' in this restricted sense that the origin of our temple should be traced. The best method which we can adopt in this investigation to secure fruitful results, is to examine these vestiges of the primitive civilization which give us a real insight into the religious beliefs of ancient peoples.

References :—

Longhurst: Report of the Arch. Dept., Southern Circle, 1915–16.

CHAPTER IV

THE STONE RING OR THE MAGIC CIRCLE

The patient labours of archæologists have brought to light thousands of graves which lie scattered all over South India and the Deccan. They belong to different ages. The earliest of them go back to what is generally called the Stone Age; and the latest belong to the 15th and 16th centuries of the Christian era. They are classified by specialists into a number of types, each of which is sharply distinguished from the others by special peculiarities of construction. The most primitive of them is, perhaps, the simple ring of stones, with three stones in the centre, marking the place where the dead body lies buried. There are hundreds of these stone-circles at Amarāvati in the Kistna district, and archæologists are of opinion that the place marks the site of the burial ground of some ancient city probably that of Dharaṇikôṭa, the eastern capital of the Ândhra kings of the Sâtavâhana dynasty. This is very probable, as stone-circles are still made use of by certain savage tribes to mark the place of burial. The Todas of the Nilgiri Hills, "even now burn their dead in a circle of stones, and bury the ashes there."[1] Generally they do not construct a new circle of stones for every corpse that is cremated; but they make use of "the same circle for repeated cremation."[2] The circle of stones that is put to this use is called by Todas an 'āzāram'; and the Toda practice of constructing 'āzārams' gives us some idea regarding the nature of the circles at Amarāvati.

We have to start our inquiry with the cemetery of Dharaṇi-kōṭa, the ancient capital of the Āndhras. Why did the people of this old city build stone-circles around the graves of their dead? Were they required to serve any real purpose? Had they any religious or other significance? What was the meaning of the three stones in the centre? It is necessary that we must find answers to all these questions, if we desire to understand them properly. To begin with, we must ascertain the meaning of the three stones in the middle of the circle. Why three stones are found in a place where one would have been sufficient is certainly a mystery, which cannot easily be unravelled. It is, however,

A stone ring at Amarāvati

Taken from Fergusson's *Indian and Eastern Architecture.*

probable that the practice of placing three stones on the graves had a simple origin. They must have been placed to prevent the ghost of the dead man rising from the grave. The stones were originally placed apart, not together, one on the head, another on the abdomen, and a third on the legs. The practice is still observed by the Bôyas, a Telugu tribe of hunters living in the hilly tracts on the western border of the Telugu districts.[a] The three stones seem to have been brought together, after the introduction of cremation. Following the Aryan practice, the Dravidians cremated the dead body, and buried the ashes; and the three stones which were originally placed in three different places on a grave were brought together, and deposited over the jar containing the ashes.*

There appears to have grown up, at the same time, a belief in the minds of men that the ghost of the dead man lives in the stones. The Khasis, a savage people that live on our eastern frontier, are accustomed to set up monoliths to honour their dead. A group of three or five, or nine is set up for every dead man whose spirit is supposed to live in it; three, however, is the most common number. The village deities who are closely related to the spirits of the dead, are similarly represented. Pôta-Râzu, the brother and sometimes the husband of Pôlêramma, is represented by three pyramidal or conical stones. Mâriyâttā is represented by three bricks in several places in the City of Madras. Three bricks represent her in Sembudas Street, just behind the University Students' Club. There is also a tiny shrine of the goddess built of earth behind the three bricks. Another group of three represents her in the Spur Tank; a third group of seven represents the deity under a tree on the Pantheon Road between the Maternity Hospital and the Museum. Another group of three bricks seen in a small shrine in the compound of the Office of the Director of the Public Instruction probably represents Munîśvara and not Mâriyâttā. In all these cases a single spirit or deity is represented by three or more stones. The number of stones does not appear to produce any disintegrating effect upon the spirit or the deity. Therefore, we cannot be far

* I happened to be present at a Brahman funeral recently. On the second day, after the pyre was extinguished and the bones of all the important joints were picked up, a rude representation of the human body was made with the ashes, and three small stones were placed upon its chest. They were then worshipped; food and clothing were offered to them. Finally they were thrown away.

from the truth, when we say that the three stones in the midst of the circle at Amarâvati represent the spirit of the dead man.

The circle of stones surrounding the three stones, or more generally the cairn has attracted much attention. Two or three theories which propose to explain its meaning have already been started. Mr. Longhurst is of opinion that the stone circles appear to be only intended as retaining walls for the earth and stones which were heaped over the stone sepulchre in the middle.[4] Mr. Longhurst's theory has an exclusive reference to the circle surrounding cairns. He ignores completely the simple stone circles, such as those that are found at Amarâvati. Moreover, his theory fails to give a satisfactory explanation even of those circles that surround the cairns. Their presence in places where they are not at all required to perform the function of 'retaining walls' destroys the theory altogether. Another hypothesis is suggested by Mr. William Crooke in his book *Things Indian*. He says, "The circle was probably intended as 'ghost-hedge,' to restrain the spirit within these assigned limits, or a sign that the site was taboo."[5] This appears to be true. The burial-ground is generally regarded as an impure place. Any one who enters it is polluted, and he requires to be purified. What is true of the burial-ground is equally true of individual graves. We find it recorded in the Ṛig-Veda that the Aryans considered the burial-ground as taboo. Ṛ.-V. X. 18 says :—

> " I place this barrier (of stones) on this
> " account that no one may go beyond it ".

More generally, however, primitive people are afraid of the spirits of the dead. It is a common belief among them that the ghosts of the dead are unhappy, and that they wreak vengeance upon the living, if they neglect them after death. They are said to be the causes of epidemics and famines. It is, therefore, necessary to propitiate them, and buy them off, by means of gifts.

The Birhors of Central India are very much troubled by the fear of evil spirits. It is said that as soon as a Birhor is dead, "his disembodied spirit becomes the prime object of fears and concern to his relatives and other people of his settlement. And the observances and ceremonies customary during this period appear to have for their main object, the prevention of harm to the tanda through his spirit on the one hand and on the other hand of harm to his spirit through stray, malignant spirits. Even the offering of food laid out for the spirit appears to be promoted less by a feeling of affection for him than from fear and a desire to keep him agreeably engaged at a distance."

Again, "the spirit of the deceased hovers about in an unsettled state between the land of the living on the one side, and spirit world on the other, and is considered peculiarly dangerous to the community as well as to itself. A woman dying within twenty-one days of child-birth, or a child dying within twenty-one days of birth, may never be admitted into the community of ancestor spirits, as their spirits are always dangerous. In their case, therefore, a new doorway to the hut is opened to take their corpses to the grave. These corpses are buried in a place apart from that where the other corpses are buried. Women and not men bury such corpses; the men only dig the graves and go away. Thorns are pricked into their feet to prevent them from leaving their graves." [6]

The Mundas of Chota Nagpur worship a set of spirits called 'banita bongas'. They consider it necessary to propitiate these spirits. The 'bonita bongas' "are indeed no gods at all, nor are they regarded by the Mundas as such. These malevolent entities . . . . are believed to be earth-bound spirits of persons who died a violent and unnatural death. The propitiation of this class of spirits is the duty—not of the Munda householder, nor of the Munda village priest, Pāhan—but of the ghost-finders. . . . . Occasionally, indeed, the earth-bound spirit of some deceased member of a family haunts his old fields and may do some mischief, and has in such a case to be propitiated by sacrifices . . . ." [7]

It is interesting to note that the Mundas who are closely related to Birhors, are in the habit of erecting rough cromlechs over the graves of their dead.

"A grave is dug at a selected spot in the Sasan (śmaśāna), and in it the earthen vessel containing the bones of the deceased is interred. Along with the bones, a little rice, oil mixed with turmeric and a few copper coins (pice) are put into a vessel. After the excavation is filled up, the large stone slab is placed upon it, supported on four small pieces of stone at the four corners." [7]

The connection between the simple circle of stones and the cromlech is well known. The latter was developed from the former, after a long process of evolution in the art of building tombs.

It is from such beliefs as have been described above that the extensive practice of worshipping the spirits of the dead arose. The true religion of the masses in South India is based upon the fear of demons with which their minds are filled. It is this fear that induced the ancient inhabitants of the land to take many precautionary steps to restrain their malignant activity. One of the steps which they adopted is to circumscribe their sphere of activity by erecting a magic circle of stones around the grave. The stone circles which form a striking feature of pre-historic graves had their origin in the need which the primitive people felt to prevent the ghosts from wandering far from the graves.

The meaning of the stone-circles at Amarâvati has been made clear by what has been said above; but these circles were not a peculiar feature of Ândhra social customs in a by-gone age. They are still erected in the Deccan and Western India in a modified form. The inhabitants of these parts are not in the habit of erecting stone-circles around the graves of the dead; but they build them in order to honour the demon, Vêtâl or Bhêtâḷa whom they commonly worship. Vêtâl is at present regarded as an *avatâra* of Śiva; but if we examine his past career, the fact that he was originally a demon becomes clear. The cult of this demon is said to be very ancient. Two arguments are generally advanced to prove its antiquity. In the first place, "Vêtâl in Deccan has no image in the shape of any animal whatever. It seems then possible that his worship was introduced previous to the custom of likening the gods to men and other animals." Secondly, "Vêtâl has no temple, but is worshipped in the open air, generally under the shade of a wide-spreading tree. This circumstance also connects his worship with the most ancient forms of idolatry."[8]

Dr. Stevenson gives us the following description of the shrine of Vêtâḷa: "The place where Vêtâl is worshipped is a kind of stone-henge or inclosure of stones, usually in somewhat of a circular shape. The following is the plan after which these circles are constructed. At some distance from the village, under a green spreading tree of any of the common indigenous species is placed Vêtâl. If as sometimes happens in a bare country like the Dekhan, no tree at a convenient distance is to be found,

Vêtâl is content to raise his head under the canopy of heaven without the slightest artificial covering whatever. The principal figure where the worship of Vêtâl is performed is a rough unhewn stone, of a pyramidal or a triangular shape placed on its base, having one of its sides fronting the east, and if under a tree, placed to the east side of the tree. The stone is of various dimensions."[9] William Crooke also gives a similar account of the circles of Vetâḷa: "In Deccan we find numerous stone-circles erected in honour of Vetâḷa, the ghost-king or the demon-lord. They are in form analogous to the European monuments of this class. The centre is occupied by a large stone in which the demon lives, and the surrounding ring his followers."[10]

The passages that have been cited show that there is a marked resemblance between the Vetâḷa circles, and the circles at the cemetery in the neighbourhood of Amarâvati. In both cases, there is a circle of stones surrounding a stone or group of three stones. We shall now proceed to examine Vetâḷa circles further, to see whether the resemblance between them and the circles at Amarâvati is only superficial, or whether there is any tie of kinship which really unites them together. The nature of Vetâḷa and the rites connected with his worship are vividly described in *Kathâ-sarit-sâgara*, a sixth century translation into Sanskṛit of the *Brihatkathā* of Guṇâḍhya, who is supposed to have lived somewhere between the 1st century B.C. and the 3rd century A.D. We understand from this work that the term Vetâḷa did not originally signify an individual demon but a class. It was applied to the ghosts of a particular type. They dwelt in cemeteries and lived upon the corpses. They could assume the forms of men or animals at will. We have a quaint description of Vetâḷa in one place: "Then came a Vetâḷa, as tall as a black palmyra tree, with the neck of a camel, the face of an elephant, the feet of a buffalo, the eyes of an owl, and the ears of a donkey."[11] But more frequently, the Vêtâḷas were believed to be ordinary ghosts which animated dead bodies. They could be pressed into the service of men, by means of powerful charms. There grew up a desire in men's minds to master them by uttering *mantras*. This desire gave birth to an extensive practice of sorcery. A person desirous of subjugating a Vetâḷa was required to perform certain preliminary rites, which were usually conducted in the *smaśāna* on the night of the fourteenth day of the dark fortnight. The undertaking was, indeed, risky, for the demon was in the habit of playing many pranks to deceive the sorcerer. If he were not courageous, he would be eaten by the demon. Many sorcerers, therefore, sought and obtained the help of heroes, in order to secure their object.

The rites that were performed in connection with the worship of Vetāḷa are described in the story of Śrī-Darśana:

> "The sorcerer adorned the corpse with red garlands and red sandal-paste; he then drew a big circle with the powder of human bones; placed in the four corners, four pots filled with human blood; lighted a lamp with the oil extracted from human fat; and making the corpse animated by Vetāḷa lie on its back in the centre of the circle, he seated himself upon its chest, and began to perform *hōma* in its mouth, using human bones as fuel." [12]

Another description of this rite is found in one of the stories of Vetāḷa:

> "He (the sorcerer) besmeared the ground with blood, and described thereon a circle with the white powder of pounded human bones; placed at the corners pots filled with blood; lighted a lamp with the oil of human fat; and by the side of it performed hôma in the fire." [13]

In another story of the same series we have a further description of this rite:

> "He (the sorcerer) helped the king to deposit the corpse on the ground. Then he gave it a bath, applied sandal paste to it, adorned it with garlands, and established it in the middle of a circle. He besmeared his body with ashes, put on a sacrificial cord of twisted hair, covered himself with a winding sheet, and meditating for a moment, he summoned by the power of his charms a Vetāḷa into the corpse, and worshipped him in accordance with the regulations. The śramaṇa gave Vetāḷa *arghya* with human blood in a human skull; offered him flowers and perfumes; gave *dhūpa* with human eyes; and offered him human flesh as a solemn meal." [14]

Yet another description:—

> "Having been thus dragged by the force of his mantras I entered the *smaśāna*, which was full of bones and skulls, surrounded by *bhūtas*, and resounding with the din caused by the cries of *bhairavas*, in a frightened condition. There I saw the *Kāpālika* who laid a corpse on its back in the middle of a circle, performing the *hōma* in the fire." [15]

In all these descriptions, two important points are noticeable: the circle of pounded human bones: and the position, in its centre, of the corpse to animate which the Vêtâḷa was summoned. The circle is the most primitive and the fundamental idea. It "acts as a prison house from which escape is impossible."[16] The ghosts of the dead are kept within this circle.

The purpose for which so many stone-circles were built in the ancient cemetery in the neighbourhood of Amarâvati has now been made clear. They were intended to restrain the ghosts from moving far from their graves. The idea that the ghosts could be pressed into the service of man came later. It was then that the sorcerers attempted to summon these ghosts into dead bodies and imprison them in a magic circle, until they promised them obedience. Vetâḷa was not the only demon that became the object of the sorcerer's magic. The Yakshas were similarly summoned to serve the masters of powerful incantations. But Vetâḷa was the most powerful and cruel of all the demons. This explains his great popularity with the magicians.

The cult of Vetāḷa, however, has undergone some modifications, since the days of Guṇâḍhya. What was originally a class name became the name of an individual demon, who is considered at the present day an *avatâra* of Śiva. The circle of pounded human bones gave place to the modern circle of stones; and the corpse disappeared to make room for the pyramidal or triangular stone in which the demon is supposed to live. The worship of an amorphous class of demons crystallized into the cult of a single devil. What was originally a temporary shrine took the shape, in course of time, of a solid and permanent circle of stones.

References :—

[1] J. W. Breeks	The Primitive Tribes of Nilgiris, p. 96.
[2] Ibid.	Ibid.
[3] Thurston	Castes and Tribes, Vol. I, p. 208.
[4] Longhurst	The Madras Archæological Report—1912-13, p. 58.
[5] William Crooke	Things Indian.
[6] S. C. Roy	The Birhors, pp. 265-67; 269-71.
[7] ,,	The Mundas, pp. 465-465.
[8] Stevenson	J. R. A. S., Vol. V, p. 192-195.
[9] ,,	Ibid.
[10] William Crooke	Things Indian.
[11] Vcnkatarâya Sâstri	Kathâ-sarit-sâgara, Vol. II, p. 869.
[12] do.	Ibid., pp. 715-16.
[13] do.	Ibid, p. 844.
[14] do.	Ibid, p. 845.
[15] do.	Ibid., pp. 1029-1030
[16] Penzer	The Ocean Story, p. 100.

CHAPTER V

THE TODA ĀZÂRAMS AND THE PRIMITIVE TEMPLES

We have suggested, in the last chapter, that the fundamental idea underlying the primitive circle of stones is the magic circle within which the sorcerer attempted to imprison ghosts. The connection between the magic circle and the shrines of Vetāḷa is also known. The shrines of Vetāḷa, however, do not help us further, in tracing the history of the South Indian temple. We have to look in other quarters for new materials. The social life of the Todas of the Nilgiris presents us certain very interesting features. It is here that we have to search for new materials. We have already referred to the Toda āzārams. It is said that at the close of the 'dry funeral,' the Todas bury the skull bone of the dead man in a corner of the Āzāram and place a block of stone over the spot. Then they bow over the stone in the Toda fashion, in order to show their respect for the dead man. The Toda āzārams are closely connected with the cairns. Breeks points out that the stone-circle is 'the fundamental idea' of cairns and barrows.

> "Now," says he, "not only may the circle of stones be called the fundamental idea of cairns and barrows, but some of them consist of insignificant circle of stones, hardly to be recognised from Toda Āzārams except by trees and bushes which indicate their greater age."[1]

The Toda Āzāram appears to be a link connecting the simple circle of stones with the cairns. The stone-circles, barrows, cairns and other kindred structures are generally attributed to a tribe of savages called Kurumbas, who dwell upon the slopes of the Nilgiri Hills. Although they do not make use of stone-circles in their funerals, it is interesting to note that they put them to a quite different use. Most of the Kurumba temples are more or less identical with the Toda Āzārams in appearance. A Kurumba temple consists of a circle of stones in the centre of which stands a block of stone. It is said that the Kurumbas worship "a rough round stone under the name of Hiriadeva, setting it up either in a cave, or in a circle of stones. . . They do not consider the stone a *lingam*, although they profess to be Śaivites."[2] According to Metz, the same deity is worshipped by the Todas

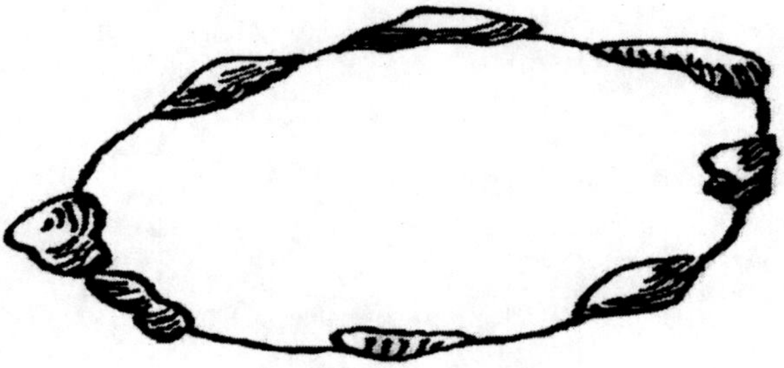

The Toda Azaram.

also. The one material object to which they offer worship is "the sacred buffalo-bell which they look upon as a representation of the deity called by them Hiriadêva, or the Chief God."[3] The temple of this god is called 'boath.' It is according to Marshall, "a building consisting of a conical thatched roof on a circular wall of very stout planking. The temple is surrounded by a massive wall of uncut stone, put together without cement, two cubits broad and three in height."[4] Within this temple Harkness found "a single stone,"[5] though there is considerable difference of opinion on this point. The structure and design of this temple are essentially the same as those of the circles at Amarâvati and the shrines of Vetāḷa. The surrounding wall of uncut stone is but the natural development of the primitive circle of rude stones. The conical temple is roughly identical in shape with the stone in which Vêtāḷa is supposed to live.*

The Irulas, another tribe dwelling on the slopes of these hills, make use of stone-circles, as temples. Although they are considerably influenced by Hindu religious ideas, their notions of temple architecture remain unaffected. "On the top of the Rangaswâmi peak, they have two temples, consisting of circles of rough stone, each enclosing an upright stone, the larger called Doḍḍa and the smaller Chikka (little) Rangaswâmi."[6] Although the stone enclosed by each circle is called Rangaswâmi, a name of Vishṇu peculiar to South India, it points to a primitive tribal deity, who became identified with Vishṇu on account of the predominant influence of Hinduism.

---

* The magic circle still clings to our temples, although its presence is not generally noticed. The following passage is very interesting :—

"One of the most important items in practices Vedic or otherwise is the Yantra. Yantra (Skt. Niyantra = binding) is any contrivance by which an entity may be bound to any spot for purposes of worship. This generally consists of geometrical figures made of metals, usually gold, silver, brass, copper, etc. In such a figure mantra, or the letters composing it, are arranged in a particular way. Such yantras are said to be the basis of idols in Hindu Temples. These yantras being made of metal can last only for a time.

"Stories are often told how idols lost their power because the yantra is worn out, or because on renewing the yantra has been made wrongly. Temples are built on yantric principles. The great temple at Sringêri Muṭṭ in Mysore Province built by Vidyāraṇya is worthy of notice It is built in the form of Srî Chakra (auspicious circle). Yantras, though popularly associated mainly with abhichāra (black magic) practices, play no inconsiderable part in the Vedic ritual . . . . ." From a booklet called "THE BHŪTAS, PRĒTAS, and PIŚĀCHAS" by R. ANANTAKRISHNA SASTRI, (p. 19).

What is said above is enough to show that the primitive stone-circles which were originally built around the graves to prevent the ghosts from going abroad and working mischief, were transformed in course of time, into the shrines of the gods whom the people worshipped. It is necessary that we should trace the growth of this process and discover the link which connects the graves with these primitive temples. We must search for it in the cult that grew very early around the graves.

In order to appease the wrath of the ghosts, people used to offer them gifts of various kinds on certain days. This resulted in the development of a cult around the graves which consequently became objects of popular worship. The practice of worshipping the graves continued even after the method of constructing the graves underwent a change. The simple stone-circles yielded place to more pretentious structures. The architecture of the graves became more complex and elaborate. Barrows and cairns which demanded greater effort and engineering skill came into existence.

The causes of this change are not clearly known. It is not possible to explain why the cairn took the place of the stone-circle. It is probable that the cairns and other elaborate tombs had their origin in the primitive habit of abandoning a house where a death had taken place after burying the corpse in it. Traces of this custom are seen in the funeral rites of the Todas. The body of a dead Toda is invariably placed in a 'funeral hut' which is generally built for the occasion. In certain Toda mounds the village dairy takes its place. All the 'funeral huts,' unless they happen to be dairies, are either abandoned or burnt down. Rivers gives us an interesting description of these huts: "In general," says he, "a funeral hut is specially built for the reception of the dead body, this hut being usually erected within a stone-circle found at the funeral place. At the funeral of a male this hut is called 'kertnodrpali' or 'neilpali.' It is left standing after the funeral, and may be used on a second occasion, if it has not fallen into too great disorder."

"At the funeral of women a hut is specially built for the reception of the body, but is always burnt down after each funeral. This hut is called 'ars' or house." [7]

The first point of interest in the above is the presence of the funeral hut in the middle of a stone-circle. The close association of the funeral hut and the stone-circle connects the latter with the primitive circles of stone which we have already described. Next, we must notice the practice of allowing a funeral hut to stand or burning it down. Even when it is allowed to stand, it is never used for any other purpose, except probably for a second funeral. The repeated use of a single hut is due to considerations of economy and convenience. The original practice was to build a separate hut for the reception of every corpse. When that was over, the hut was abandoned or burnt down. Lastly, the names of these huts themselves betray their original connection with dwelling houses: huts built for the reception of corpses of women are called 'ars' or house; whereas those that are built for men are called 'pāli,' a word which also means 'a dairy.' Now, the dairy is closely related to the funeral hut. "Among some sections of the Todas, the body is placed, not in a funeral hut, but in a dairy before the last rites."[8] In others, the funeral hut is built on the model of dairies with three rooms. It is clear from this that the funeral huts built for males are somehow connected with dairies. The early Todas were a wandering tribe of pastoral nomads. Their wealth consisted of their herds of buffaloes; their chief business in life was the management of their dairies; in fact, the dairy was the place where their life activity was concentrated. Therefore, when a man of the community died, he was buried in his dairy which was subsequently abandoned.

The funeral hut appears to be related to the cairns, for the hill tribes of the Nilgiris call them *sâvu-mane* or 'houses of death.' This view gains strength from the remarks of Dr. Hunt who points out that the ancient graves were built on the model of human habitations.[9]

What gave solidity and permanence to the funeral hut appears to be the development of new religious ideas. The cairn-builder was "a firm believer in after-life." Perhaps, he believed like the Toda that the people in the other world "live in much the same way as the inhabitants of this world."[10] He thought, therefore, that "whatever is necessary, useful and ornamental in this world would be equally so in the next—the warrior would require his sword, the husbandman his agricultural implements."[11] In order to provide for the needs of the dead in the other world, the cairn-builder stocked the tomb with all articles of "food and drink, cooking pots and weapons."[12] To secure their safety, he built it with solid granite blocks, below the surface of the earth.

Breeks draws attention to this process of transition among the pre-historic graves upon the Nilgiris. He shows that Toda Āzârams approximate to the cairns and that the barrows are closely connected with the cromlechs.[13] As the art of sepulchral architecture develops, the stone-circles show a tendency to disappear, although they continue to be erected around the cairns and the cromlechs occasionally. The fact that the cairns and allied structures are graves is shown by the name which is given them by the people upon the hills. They are called *sâvu-mane* 'houses of death.' Occasionally, the savage Kurumbas of the hills still make use of "chromlechs for burial purposes, and place the long water-worn pebble in it."[14] According to Walhouse the pebble is called '*deva kotta kallu*';[15] and is supposed to represent the spirit of the dead man.

Some of these funeral monuments are still worshipped by people in certain places. We are indebted to Metz for describing a cairn which is regularly worshipped by the Kurumbas:

> "I was once on a preaching excursion in a district near the southern boundary of the hills, and not far from the Kurumba village, called Mulli, and after the labours of the day felt a curiosity to open a cairn which happened to be in the neighbourhood. Much to my surprise, however, the Badaga headmen present would not permit me to do so, not on account of any objection they had themselves to make, but because as they said, it was the residence of the god of the Kurumbas who came up frequently from Mulli, in order to worship the god of their forefathers. This is the only occasion on which I have ever known any of the hill tribes venerate a cairn as the depository of the ashes of a dead ancestor." [16]

The Malei-Ariyans (Malai-araiyans) of Travancore, according to Walhouse, "make miniature cromlechs of small slabs of stone and place within them a long pebble to represent the dead. . . . (They) offer arak (liquor) and sweetmeats to the departed spirit" [17] which is supposed to hover near the miniature cromlech.

The Kurumbas and the Malei-Ariyans are not the only people who worship the cairns and the cromlechs. The other tribes dwelling on the Nilgiri Hills do the same. Each Badaga community keeps, according to Breeks, "a Kurumba priest called Kāni-kurumba (Kanik). . . . The office is hereditary. In April

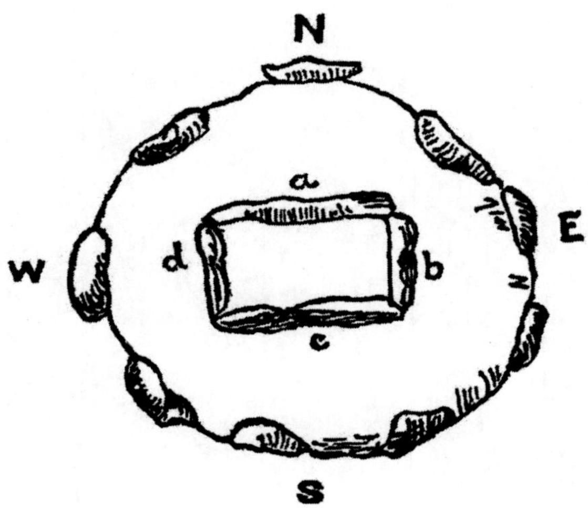

A Cairn.

and May before the sowing time, a goat or young buffalo is supplied by the cultivators, and the Kani-kurumba is summoned to make the sacrifice. Surrounded by the villagers, the officiating priest cuts off the head of the animal, and sprinkles the blood in three directions, east, west and south, and also on a water-worn stone which is considered a 'hûtu (natural)—lingam' (*huttu-lingam*). . . . In Jatakanêri-grâma, this ceremony is performed at a cromlech; in Tênad at a rude circle of stones surrounding a water-worn stone for lingam. They call the place the Kurumba-kovil (the Kurumba Church)." [18] In addition to this, the Badagas worship at a large number of cromlechs. Speaking of the monuments of this class, Walhouse expresses the opinion that although their original intention was undoubtedly sepulchral, he does not feel certain that it was so with respect to some of them.[19] Breeks states his opinion more definitely: "They may have been purely memorial, and have contained only perishable offerings of rice &c. such as are made by the Kurumbas and the Kols of Chota Nagpur."[20]

This is probable. In that case, we have here an instance where a structure which was originally worshipped as a sepulchre is divorced from its original purpose and put to a novel use. The grave is thus transformed into a temple, although the atmosphere of the graveyard still clings to it.

The cromlechs or 'soul-houses,' as Mr. Longhurst calls them, are seen all over South India. They usually consist "of one large flat slab of stone supported by three upright slabs set on end or on edge so as to form a small chamber with one side open to serve as an entrance. They have been erected as special abodes for the ghosts of the departed, and also as votive offerings made by the survivors to propitiate the spirits of the dead."[21]

Mr. Longhurst selects two of these to illustrate an important stage in the development of the South Indian temple, when the simple 'soul-house' was transformed into the abode of the deity. At Kambadur a village in the Kalyandrug taluk of the Anantapur district, there stand "three very interesting old dolmens which have been set up as Śiva shrines."[22] Mr. Longhurst is of opinion that we may find here the prototype of the so-called Dravidian or ordinary South Indian type of Hindu temple.[23] He proceeds to describe these shrines at some length. As it is very important in connection with the following discussion, we take the liberty of quoting him in full.

"In plate III Fig. (a) we have two examples of these Śiva shrines standing close together, the one in the foreground is much the same in size and style as the large dolmen shown in plate I Fig. (a), only it has been converted into a Śiva's temple by the introduction of a stone linga surrounded by a low flat yoni-pedestal of early type, and a drainage hole for the exit of the holy water poured over the linga, had been cut through the same slab forming the north wall of the shrine as may be seen in plate IV (a). At a short distance to the south-west of this shrine, we have no longer a primitive dolmen but a carefully built temple enshrining a tall stone linga on a yoni-pedestal of the usual type. The three side walls and the roof are not built of roughly hewn slabs, as we find in the earlier example, but consist of four large slabs of stone carefully cut and dressed, and accurately fitted at the angles. The side walls rest upon a moulded plinth about one foot in height, and are not planted in the ground like the wall slabs of a dolmen. . . . .

"At a short distance to the south-east of these two shrines is the dolmen-temple illustrated in plate III Fig. (b) and plate IV (b). This also is a Śiva shrine containing a stone linga and yoni-stand like the others just mentioned. The construction of the stone chamber is similar to the dolmen-temple shown in plate III Fig. (a). Only here the shrine chamber has been provided with a hall or mantapa in front connected with the shrine by a small passage, the entire structure being roofed with three roughly-hewn flat slabs of granite. The plan of the building is the usual kind for the small Hindu temples in the so-called Dravidian style."[24]

Mr. Longhurst is quite right in his supposition that the Kambadur group of dolmen shrines 'represents the ordinary South Indian type of Hindu temple,' although it may be doubted whether they were originally dedicated to god Śiva. The presence of a cylindrical stone in the sanctum of a temple need not necessarily mean that the temple is dedicated to Śiva. In spite of the great importance that is attached to this group, it does not properly represent the transition stage in the development of the South Indian temple so well as some of the primitive monuments existing in the country. In the Ceded Districts, the dolmen country par excellence, there lives a community of primitive people called Kurubas whose racial identity with the Kurumbas of the Nilgiris has been well established. Like the Kurumbas, they worship the graves where the spirits of the dead are supposed to dwell. Some of these graves have developed in course of time into big shrines. These shrines of the Kurubas are representative of the South Indian temple during the period of transition. That this is so is clearly shown by the following description :—

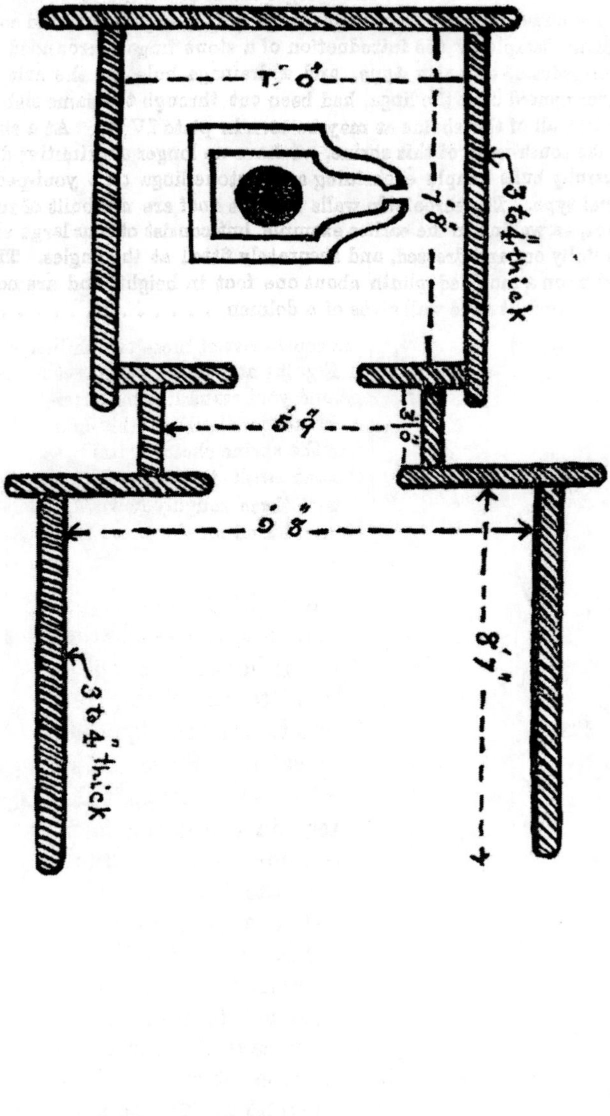

Taken from the *Archæological Report.* *Southern Circle.* 1915–16.

The Graves of the Curubaru.

Taken from *The Castes and Tribes*, Vol. IV.

The Shrine of Bir Dêvaru

From *The Castes and Tribes*, Vol. IV.

"The temples of this caste," says Thurston, "are usually rather extensive, but rude low structures resembling an enclosed mantapam supported by rough stone-pillars, with a small inner shrine, where the idols are placed during the festival time. A wall of stone encloses a considerable space round the temple, and this is covered with small structures formed of four flat stones, three being the walls and the fourth the roof. The stone facing the open side has a figure sculptured upon it, representing the deceased Gaudu or Pujari to whom it is dedicated. For each person of rank, one of these monuments is erected, and here periodically, and always during the annual feasts puja is made not only to the spirits of the deceased chiefs, but also to those of all who have died in the clan. It seems impossible not to connect this with those strange structures called by natives Pandava's temples." [25]

This description is very important for our purpose, for it is the real link that connects the cromlechs of the Nilgiris with the Hindu temples of South India. In the first place, it clearly demonstrates that the grave and the temple are very closely connected, and that the latter is a development of the former. The kinship of the graves of Gauḍas with the so-called Pāṇḍava's temples is admitted; but the relationship between the graves of the Gauḍas and the shrine in the interior is not pointed out. The design and the general plan of construction are same in both the cases. "The temple," in the words of Thurston, "resembles a mantapam supported upon rough stone pillars, with a small inner shrine." The only difference between this and the graves of the Gauḍas is that in the former, four corner pillars take the place of three granite blocks supporting the roof. If we compare the Kurumba temple on p. 153 of Vol. IV of the *Castes and Tribes* with the pictures of Kurumba graves on page 155 of the same volume, the kinship of the Kurumba shrine with the graves of the Gauḍas on the one hand, and the striking resemblance of the latter to the cromlechs on the other become at once evident. That the shrine of the Kurumba god is connected with their dead heroes is corroborated by the nature of the god himself. He is called 'Bīra-Dêvaru,' which means 'a hero-god.'

"The Curubaru (of Mysore) believe," says Buchanan, "that those men who die without having been married become Vīrikas to whose images, at a great annual feast which is celebrated on purpose, offerings of red cloth, jaggery, rice, &c., are made. If this feast be omitted, the Vîrikas become enraged, occasion sickness, kill the sheep, alarm the people by horrid dreams and when they walk out at night strike them on the back. They are only to be appeased by the celebration of the proper feast."[26]

The term 'Vîrika' also means 'a hero.' The 'Bîra-Dêvaru' is none other than the universalised spirit of a departed Kuruba. It is quite natural that his shrine should resemble the graves and be surrounded by them.

Secondly, we must notice the wall of stone, which "encloses a considerable space round the temple." This wall also reminds us of cairns and cromlechs. It is the primitive circle of stones surrounding the pre-historic graves in a developed form. Although the circle of stones tended to disappear generally with the development of sepulchral architecture, it survived in certain places. In the Mysore country, some of the dolmens are surrounded by stone-circles. We have already noticed that in the case of the Toda 'boath,' it had taken the shape of the surrounding wall. There is one peculiarity of some of the Mysore dolmens which must be noted. They have "arch stones on the entrance-side at the inner edge of the stone circles. These arches are thin slabs of dark stone, roughly shaped by hammer-dressing into a rounded arch. . . . . In east Mysore dolmens are found enclosed by four great arch-shaped slabs 9′ or 10′ high, set up parallel to, and a little apart from, the four walls of the dolmen." [27]

These features of the ancient funeral monuments have passed, in course of ages, into our temple architecture. The *prākāra* and the gates which form the prominent features of the South Indian temples have come down to us from the graveyards of pre-historic times.

The rude shrine of Bîra-Dêvaru thus presents many points of interest to the student of ancient institutions. A more searching investigation of this institution is well worth the trouble.

References:

[1] Breeks ... ... The Primitive Tribes of Nilgiris, pp. 96–7.

[2] Do. ... ... Ibid., p. 53.

[3] F. Metz. ... ... The Tribes Inhabiting the Nilgiri Hills, p. 17.

[4] William E. Marshal. A Phrenologist Amongst the Todas, p. 163.

[5] Harkness, Henry — A Singular Aboriginal Race, p. 22.
[6] J. W. Breeks — The Primitive Tribes, p. 70.
[7] Rivers ... — Todas, pp. 338–40.
[8] Do. ... — Ibid.
[9] Dr. Hunt — Journal of the Hyderabad Archæological Society, 1916 July, pp. 221–2.
[10] Rivers ... — Todas, p. 398.
[11] Maurice Philips — Ind. Anti., Vol. II, p. 228.
[12] Dr. Hunt — Journal of the Hyderabad Arch. Society, 1916, July, pp. 221–2.
[13] J. W. Breeks — The Primitive Tribes, pp. 96–97, 108.
[14] Do. — Ibid.
[15] M. J. Walhouse — Ind. Ant., Vol. II, p. 276.
[16] F. Metz ... — Tribes Inhabiting the Nilgiri Hills, p. 125.
[17] M. J. Walhouse — Ind. Ant., Vol. VI, p. 4.
[18] J. W. Breeks — The Primitive Tribes, pp. 53–4.
[19] M. J. Walhouse — Ind. Ant., Vol. II, p. 276.
[20] J. W. Breeks — The Primitive Tribes, p. 105.
[21] Longhurst — Annual Report of Arch. Dept., Southern Circle, 1915–16.
[22] Do. — Ibid.
[23] Do. — Ibid.
[24] Do. — Ibid.
[25] E. Thurston — The Castes and Tribes, Vol. IV.
[26] Buchanan — Travels &c., Vol. I, pp. 275–6.
[27] G. S. Ghurye — Man in India, Vol. VI, p. 48.

CHAPTER VI

THE PRIMITIVE TEMPLE AND THE TEMPLE OF THE VILLAGE DEITY

We began, in the first chapter, with the statement that the gods and goddesses of the original inhabitants of Southern India had no temples. Next, we traced the development of temples from the graves of the departed heroes and chiefs belonging to the pre-historic times; but these temples had no connection whatsoever with any of the gods whom the people worshipped. We know from literature and inscriptions that from very early times our gods and goddesses were housed in very large temples. How did this happen? How did these gods and goddesses come to live in temples? This is the problem to which we have to find a solution. Once again, we must start from the graveyard; but it must be noted here that the spirits of the dead, with whom the temple in early days was very closely associated, are quite different from the gods.

The passage which we have quoted in a previous context from Buchanan contains the solution which we are in search of. He describes a belief current among the Kurubas of Mysore, according to which a certain class of dead men becomes Vîrikas. Now, Vîrika is not a mere demon, but he has also a divine aspect. The Vîrikas, therefore, are the spirits that are on the borderland between the heaven of the gods and the land of the demons.

The Kurubas are not the only people who believe in the Vîrikas. The Idigas, the Gollas, the Boyas, and a number of other tribes hold similar beliefs. Here we are introduced to a phase of religion which exhibits a tendency to obliterate the distinction between the demon and the deity. The obliteration of difference becomes complete in the cult of the village deities. A large number of these deities, especially in the Ândhradeśa, begin their career from the confines of the graveyard. In course of time, their origin is forgotten, and they are established as powerful deities. Dr. Elmore is of opinion that "the gods of the Dravidians are almost universally human beings returned to earth."[1] We cannot agree with Dr. Elmore to the total extent of his

The temple of the village deity.

From Whitehead's *Village Deities*.

contention, although we can understand how he arrived at the above conclusion. The facts that forced on him this conclusion, are connected with the history of a number of the so-called Dravidian deities. We shall consider some of them as specimens. We begin with Kanaka-Durgamma, the goddess presiding over the destinies of the town of Bezwada. She is very well known over the whole of the Āndhra country.

The origin of the goddess is described as follows:—"There were seven Brahman brothers in a village, who had one sister Kanakamma. Her conduct filled them with suspicion, and when she heard their state of mind, she drowned herself in a well. The people of the village feared a police investigation, and they started the story that Kanakamma had become a Śakti and entered the hills.

"The story that Kanakamma had become a goddess was not so easily stopped as was the investigation. When the body was taken from the well and buried, the people began to worship her at that place, and soon built her a temple." [2]

Another village deity, Lingamma has the following story associated with her origin: "In Mupparâzuvâripâḷem, Darsi taluk, Nellore district, lived a woman called Lingamma. She was of the Śūdra caste, but she and her husband were poor, and worked in the house of a rich man of the same caste. Once some valuables were missing from the house, and suspicion pointed to Lingamma. Her employer made her much trouble, and was about to take legal proceedings against her, when she ended the matter by jumping into the well and drowning herself.

"A few days after this tragic death, troubles began to come to the household of her employer. A little later Lingamma appeared to him twice in a dream, and told him that because of his cruelty, she was bringing these troubles upon him. She also threatened him with worse disasters, if he did not institute a proper worship for her. His response evidently was not satisfactory, for Lingamma immediately brought a scourge of cholera upon the village, and appeared to many as a devil. All were now thoroughly frightened, and led by Lingamma's former employer, they built a temple of some importance, and prepared an image of both Lingamma and her husband, and instituted the worship already described."[3]

The story of Podilamma, the tutelary goddess of the village of Podili in the Nellore District runs as follows :—" Some Śūdra farmers lived in a hamlet at some distance from the present village of Podili. One day they were treading out the grain with the oxen in a distant field. Their sister was to bring them the mid-day meal. On the way in a lonely place, she met a man. She put down her basket, and was late in arriving with food. When she arrived, her brothers caught her and threw her beneath the feet of oxen, for they had been watching her while she came, and believed her to be guilty.

" The girl, evidently killed, disappeared under the feet of the cattle among the sheaves. Later when they removed the straw to winnow the grain, they did not find the body, but found a stone. A man standing near became possessed with the spirit of the girl, and she spoke through him. She said that she had been killed unjustly, and that they must worship her, or great evils would follow. All the people who heard this were terrified, and placing the stone in a desirable place, they began its worship."[4] The fame of Podilamma increased, and she became the goddess presiding over the village of Podili. The history of a host of other village deities such as Buchamma, Lodạthamma, Gonti, &c., is similar.

It appears from what has been said above that it is only women that become deities after death. This is generally the case; but there are certain notable instances, where men also become famous as deities. In a village in the Kandukur taluk, there lived a Mâdiga who " knew many mantrams, and all the people stood in great fear of him.[4] . . . He established illicit relations with a caste woman, the daughter of a rich man." The father of the girl who naturally disliked his daughter's illicit connection with the low caste man, lured him at midnight into the temple of Poleramma, and had him murdered. Soon after the murder, many troubles came upon the villagers. " Some of the people went mad, and some children and cattle suddenly sickened and died. The villagers approached a diviner who became possessed with the spirit of the dead Mâdiga and demanded worship. But they said, ' Chee ! Would we worship a Mâdiga ? ' Their troubles continued, and they finally agreed to worship him as a deity."[5]

The reputation of this Mâdiga deity is confined to a few villages. It pales into insignificance when compared to Kôṭappa Koṇḍasvâmi who had a similar origin. "The legend runs that about one hundred years ago, a man named Yellamanda Kôṭiah, of the Linga Balija division of the Śūdra caste ruined the wife of a shepherd when she was herding the cattle on the hill. The deed became known to her husband, and he determined to seek revenge. The next day, he went himself to herd the cattle, and when Kôṭiah came expecting the woman as usual, her husband fell upon him, and killed him. He also killed his wife near the same spot.

"Soon after this, the villagers heard a voice rising from the place where the blood fell. The voice threatened them with death, if they did not build a temple and institute worship for the murdered man whose blood was crying to them from the ground. The temple was built for Kôṭiah to whom the name of Kôṭappa Koṇḍasvâmi is now given. A shrine was erected to the murdered woman who is now worshipped as a Śakti." [6]

The fame of Kôṭappa Koṇḍasvâmi has spread over the whole of the Telugu country, and he is even identified with Śiva. The origin of this deity isal most forgotten, and people visit the temple built over the grave of Kôṭiah merely as a shrine dedicated to Śiva. The evolution of gods from human beings appears to be an old process. The poet Śrînâtha who lived in the fourteenth century makes the following observation regarding the religion of Palnâḍ:

" ఉ. వీరులు దివ్య లింగములు - విష్ణువు చెన్నుఁడు కల్లుపోతురా
జారయకాల భైరవుఁడు - నంకమశక్తియు నన్నపూర్ణ."

"The heroes are the divine *lingas*; Chenna is Vishṇu. On enquiry Kālabhairava is found to be Kallu-Pôturāju; Ankamma, the Śakti, is Annapūrna." [7]

These instances are sufficient to illustrate the point. The tendency to identify the spirits of those who die under exceptional circumstances with the village deities is common. The conclusion that "gods of the Dravidians are almost universally human beings returned to earth" appears to be just. However, anyone drawing such a conclusion yields to a great temptation. It is not true that the Dravidian gods are always 'human beings returned to earth.' The great Śaktis in whom almost every Hindu in South India believes are certainly not 'human beings returned to earth.' This is shown by the presence, in a number of villages, of *grâmadêvatās* who have altogether no connection with the dead. In these villages the *grâmadêvatā* is simply called 'Ûramma or the village-mother.' There are no legends connected with her except that she is one of the seven sisters and a wife of Śiva. No doubt, the spirits of a certain class of the dead are identified with the village deities. That does not mean that the Śaktis themselves had a human origin. The truth is that the divine aspect of a dead person becomes one with the Śaktis; hence the identification. We cannot understand this clearly, unless we forget all the advanced ideas which we associate with our notions of the deity. It is not at all necessary that a god or goddess should be only good. The Dravidian deities are not particular about the ethical distinction between good and evil. It is the idea of power that is emphasized in them. They are the embodiments of power. They may be good or they may be evil. It is not of very great consequence. What really matters is power. Our *grâmadêvatās* generally do evil to mankind. It is not due to their love of wickedness that they act in this fashion, but to the desire to exhibit their power. It is the only way in which men can understand and respect power. No amount of good can convince men that the gods are powerful and strong. It is necessary that men should understand that the gods are powerful enough to harm them, and strong enough to protect them. This view is further strengthened by the following consideration. The word which signifies a devil in Telugu is '*dayyamu.*' The same word is employed to signify 'god' also. The primitive Āndhras, therefore, could not have distinguished the god from the devil. What they could understand and appreciate was power. Therefore, they called every supernatural being '*dayyamu,*' irrespective of all ethical considerations.

The preceding discussion has shown that the spirits of the departed have a strong affinity to the village deities with whom they become identified. We have tried to explain the cause of that identification. Now, it is easy for us to understand how the temple which grew around the grave was transferred to the village deities. It is brought about by the association of the dead with the village deities. The primitive people are in the habit of grouping together a number of religious rites, on account of economic considerations. We are told that the Todas "hold the Marvainolkedr of several people at the same time."[8] This is due to considerations of rural economy. The Kurubas of the Ceded Districts hold a feast once a year in honour of all the dead of the clan during the year. In small village communities which are required to celebrate feasts in honour of ancestral spirits as well as the village deities, the tendency is to bring both feasts together in order to minimise expense. In some of our most important annual feasts, we find a combination of two kinds of worship.

The Dīpâvaḷī is celebrated with great enthusiasm in the South. The New Year of the Gujarâtis and Mârwâris begin with that Amâvâsyâ. At one time, Dīpâvaḷī must have been specially sacred to the ancient spirits. In the Tamil country all the non-Brahmans fast and worship the ancestors on that day. The preceding day, the fourteenth day of the black fortnight, is called Naraka-chaturdaśī or 'the fourteenth day of hell.' Crackers are fired to scare away the evil spirits. The Dīpâvaḷī, therefore, seems to be an 'all-souls' day.' The worship of ancestral spirits is closely associated with the worship of the deities of vegetation. The Kêdâreśvara-vrata is performed on the day succeeding the Dīpâvaḷī. Kêdâreśvara is the 'lord of the fields,' and his worship usually takes place in the midst of paddy-fields.

The Pongal is mainly a feast celebrated in honour of the goddess of vegetation, Gaurī. Her worship continues for one week in the month of Pushya. The Telugu year used to terminate at one time with the Pongal; for the last day of the feast is still called *Èḍādi-panḍuga* 'the new-year feast.' On this day, all the Āndhras with the exception of the Brahmans fast and worship the ancestors.

Now, the worship of two sets of deities at the same time leads naturally to a combination of the two cults. Their attributes and qualities become interchangeable. The temple which originally belonged to the spirits of the dead has been thus transferred to the village deities. This fact is clearly shown by the legends and rites associated with the village deities and the presence of their temples in *śmaśânas*.

"Among the Śaktis, Kāṭi Ankamma is one of considerable importance. She is the Śakti of the place where the dead are buried or burned, and is feared accordingly."[9]

The worship of this deity lasts only for a short duration, "for it is not pleasant enough to be extended any longer than is necessary. The Mâdiga story-teller goes to the burial-ground accompanied by the people in whose interest the worship is conducted."[10] Kâṭi Ankamma, therefore, dwells in the *kâḍu* or 'the cremation ground.'

Another Śakti, Ankāḷamma, lives within the precincts of the *śmaśâna.* "At Malayânur, a ceremony called 'Mayâna (śmaśâna)-koḷḷai' (looting the burning ground) is performed. The village of Malayânur is famous for its Ankâḷamman temple, and during the festival which takes place immediately after Śivarâtri, some thousands of people congregate at the temple, which is near the burning ground. . . ."[11]

Another goddess who bears distinct marks of her residence in the *śmaśâna* is Muttyâlamma or 'the pearl-like mother.' We have a picture of this deity on p. 225 of *the South Indian Images of Gods and Goddesses* of H. Krishna Sastri. She is here seated crossing her left leg and extending the right below, so that her right foot may rest upon the chest of a dead body. She wears many ornaments, the most significant of which is the necklace of skulls. The corpse and the necklace point to her usual place of habitation.

Literature bears ample testimony to the existence of temples of Kâḷi or Durgā in the *śmaśâna*. The *Kathāsaritsāgara* of Somadeva contains a description of a temple of Durgā at Benares. The temple was situated outside the town. There was a *śmaśâna* in its neighbourhood. People could see the burning pyres from the temple as Govindasvāmi and his son Vijayadatta had done.

The poet Bhavabhûti also describes a temple of Durgā situated in a *śmaśâna* in his *Mâlatî-Mâdhava*. The heroine Mâlatî is led to the temple of Châmuṇḍā to be sacrificed. "The temple is situated in the burning ground."[12] The hero, Mâdhava, goes there to secure human flesh which he requires in performing some Tântric rites; and finding his beloved bound and ready to be offered as a sacrifice, rescues her.

The Temple of Durga at Mahābalipura

From Havell's *Indian Architecture*.

Hut-urns

We have another description of a Kāḷi's temple in a *śmaśāna*, in the Tamil poem *Maṇi-mēkhalai.* Here is the description of the burning ground: "The burning ground which is adjacent to the grove is as old as the city itself. It is surrounded by a high wall, which has four main gates in it. The gate which has the flag-staff is for the *dēvas*, who leave the cars standing in mid-air looking like painted pictures, and enter through it. Then there is the stately entrance, the sides of which are adorned with beautiful pictures of paddy-fields, sugar-canes, tanks and groves. The third gate has bare white-washed walls, while in the front of the fourth stands the terrible image of a demoness, fiercely frowning and biting her lips, and holding the fatal noose and spear in her hands. Soldiers guard this enclosure. It is haunted by devils. Within the walls are seen many strange sights, and terrific sounds are heard here. There you can see the great temple of Kāḷi, with the altar in the front yard surrounded by lofty trees which bend down with the weight of the heads of those who have sacrificed themselves to the goddess." [13]

These instances confirm the view that the village deities have borrowed their temples from the ghosts of the cemetery. A comparison of the hut-urns with the temples of *grāmadēvatas* leads us to the same conclusion. The 'hut-urns' or urns shaped like huts were used in ancient times for burying the ashes of the dead. A good number of them have been unearthed by archæologists. They resemble very closely a class of temples dedicated to the village deities. Bruce Foote tells us that he saw 'a very small but typical hut-urn. . . . . in the fields a couple of miles or so to the east of Salem.' It "was in use as a shrine of some swāmi, who would in consideration of a lamp burning to his or her hut-urn, take care of the crops growing in front." [14]

Now, the Salem hut-urn links the hut-shaped temples of village deities with the hut-urn properly so called, which takes us once again into the precincts of the graveyard. A picture of a perfect hut-urn dug out of the soil of India is not available; but we are able to get a representation of its European prototype There is little or no difference between the two. The Indian hut-urns "show a resemblance to the same objects of Western classical antiquity, such as were found under the volcanic turfa near the Alban lakes to the south of Rome." [15]

Again, we arrive at the same conclusion, when we compare another class of *grāmadēvata* shrines with the dolmens. One of the dolmens of the Kambadur group III (*b*) admirably serves our purpose. "The construction of the shrine chamber is similar to the dolmen temples. . . Only here the shrine chamber has been provided with a hall or mantapa in front connected with the shrine by a small passage; the entire structure being roofed with three roughly hewn flat slabs of granite." [16] The resemblance between this and the plan of the South Indian temple is generally admitted. Nowhere is this resemblance more striking than in the case of the temples of the village deities. The ground plan and the superstructure are the same in both the cases. The temple of the village deity is generally oblong in form. From outside, it appears as a single hall, having no doorway and generally no windows. The roof is a flat terrace, and is not adorned by images. When we enter the temple, however, we find that what appears from outside, as a single hall, is really divided into two chambers, one in front, and another behind it. These two chambers correspond with the mantapam and the shrine of the Kambadur dolmen temple. This type of the temple of the village deity, therefore, must have had its origin in the primitive dolmen.

The transference of rites and ceremonies belonging to the dead to the village deities is nowhere seen more clearly than in the history of the Car. It originally formed part of funeral rites. The custom of building funeral cars survives still among a number of South Indian communities. It appears to be quite popular with the Billavas and the Bants of the West Coast. Among the Billavas, the final death ceremonies (or *bojja*) are performed on the thirteenth day. "On the evening of the previous day, at the place where the dead person breathed his last, a small bamboo car, in three tiers, is constructed, and decorated with coloured cloths. This car is called 'Nirneralu.' A lamp is suspended from the car, and a cot placed on the ground beneath it, and the jewels and clothes of the dead person are laid thereon." The next day "the various articles are collected, and tied up in a bundle, which is placed in a palanquin, and carried in a procession by two to the *upparige*, which has been constructed over the *dhūpe*." The car is also taken, evidently, to the cremation ground. "Those present go thrice round the *upparige*, and the chief mourner unties the bundle, and places its contents on the car." "All the present then leave the spot, and the barber removes the cloths from the car, and pulls it down. Sometimes, if the dead person has been an important member of the community, a small car is constructed, and taken in procession round the *upparige*."[17]

Here, the car is made to serve its original purpose. It is constructed in connection with the funeral rites of an individual; and it is pulled down when they are over. The same practice is observed by the Badagas of the Nilgiri Hills. "The funeral car is built up in five to eleven tiers, decorated with clothes and streamers, and one tier must be covered with black chintz." "The corpse is carried to the car, and placed in the lowest storey thereof (on a cot), washed, dressed in coat and turban." "When all are assembled, the cot is carried to an open space between the house and the burning ground, followed by the car." "The car is then stripped of its trappings and hacked to pieces." Here also the car appears to be a mere appendage of a funeral. It is built for the funeral of a single individual, and is destroyed immediately after it has served its purpose. The Badagas, however, put it also to a different use, in connection with the celebration of the memorial ceremony for ancestors called '*manavalai*.' The festival "takes place at long intervals." "An enormous car, called *elu-kuḍi-tēru* (seven-storeyed car) was built of wood and bamboo and decorated with silk and woollen fabrics, flags and umbrellas. Inside the ground floor were a cot with a mattress and pillow, and the stem of a plantain tree. The souls of the ancestors were supposed to be reclining on the cot, resting their heads on the pillow, and chewing the plantains, while the umbrellas protect them from the sun and rain. The ear ornaments of all those who have died since the previous ceremony should be placed upon the cot." After much dancing and merry-making which continued for days, "the cot was eventually burnt at the burning-ground, as if it contained a corpse."[18]

The car is not built here, as in the two previous cases for use in actual funerals. It is constructed on the occasion of a memorial ceremony for ancestors. It has here assumed a religious significance.

We see the car again associated with the village deities. In Orissa, a car is constructed "for the annual festival of the village deity, at which, in most places, the car is burnt at the conclusion of the festival."[19]

Here the car has no connection with the dead or the funerals. But it appears to be connected with the Badaga car built for *manavalai*. It is built like the Badaga car to be used in a recurring festival, and it is burnt down as soon as it is over.

The three instances that have been cited above show how the car which is originally a mere appendage of funerals at first transforms itself into an institution connected with ancestral worship, and finally enters into the rites connected with the celebration of the annual festival of village deities.

When new gods invaded South India from the North they entered these temples, making alliances in most cases with their original occupants. The South Indian temple which started its career as a rude circle of stones around a grave, ended by becoming the abode of the mighty gods of the conquering Aryan religion.

References :—

[1] Dr. Elmore ... The Dravidian Gods in Hindu Religion.
[2] " ... Ibid.
[3] " ... Ibid.
[4] " ... Ibid.
[5] " ... Ibid.
[6] " ... Ibid.
[7] Prabhākara Śāstrulu Chāṭu Verses, p. 125.
[8] Rivers ... The Todas, p. 372.
[9] Dr. Elmore ... The Dravidian Gods, etc.
[10] Thurston ... Castes and Tribes, Vol. VI, p. 356.
[11] Penzer ... Tawney's translation of Katha-sarit-sagara, Vol. II pp. 196–7.
[12] " ... Ibid., p. 214.
[13] A. Madhaviah ... Maṇimēkhalai, pp. 34–37.
[14] Bruce Foot ... Indian Pre-historic and Proto-historic Antiquities, p. 85.
[15] " ... Ibid.
[16] Longhurst ... Report of Arch. Southern Circle, 1915–16.
[17] Thurston ... Castes and Tribes, Vol. I, p. 250.
[18] " ... Ibid., pp. 112–123.
[19] " ... Ibid., p. 128.

CHAPTER VII

THE ORIGIN OF THE VIMANA

We have confined our attention, so far, to a consideration of the ground plan and the basal structure of the South Indian temple. We have purposely ignored an important feature of the temple architecture. It is the imposing *vimâna* that is built on the temple, just above the sanctum. Whence has it come? We have not been able to detect even a trace of it in the primitive Dravidian temple. Its origin is, therefore, shrouded in darkness. Some people are inclined to see in it a foreign element; some trace its origin to the Egyptian Pyramids; others find in it an adaptation of Chaldean Ziggarets. The most important of the theories explaining the origin of the *vimâna* comes from Mr. Longhurst. His theory is as follows:—

The *stûpi*, as the *vimâna* is called, is the corrupted form of Sanskrit *stûpa* which signifies 'a Buddhistic shrine.' It was originally "a dome-shaped structure which was a development of the low sepulchral tumulus, or mound of earth and stones, in which the bricks were substituted for earth, with a view to durability."[1] The Buddhists did not, however, bring the *stûpa* into existence. It existed long before the time of the Buddha. It was a pre-Buddhistic institution, held in great reverence by the people. It was "a common form of tomb at that period" and "nothing more or less than a regularly built dome-shaped pile of masonry, which was undoubtedly the oldest form of funeral monuments."[2] To secure the loyalty of the masses, the Buddha is said to have adopted it for the purpose of his new religion. And after the death of the master, it was further developed and universalised by his followers, and it became 'the' religious edifice of the Buddhists. "A striking change in the mediaeval *stûpa* is the introduction of figure-sculpture. Only ordinary mortals are sculptured in the earlier *stûpas*, while Buddha never appears. Now he is even the object of worship, his image being placed in a niche in front of the *stûpa* itself."[3] It was this developed Buddhistic *stûpa* which the Hindus adopted as their temple when Buddhism began to decay. The Hindus had no temples before this period. The earliest representations of the Hindu deities are found on Buddhist temples. "The oldest remains of independent Hindu art either sculptural or architectural only date from several centuries after the beginning of our (the Christian) era. These considerations in themselves justify the presumption that Hindu architecture is derived from the older art of the Buddhists."[4]

So far, everything appears to run smooth; but there emerges a difficulty when this theory has to be adapted to the South Indian temple, on account of its independent origin. We have already seen that the South Indian temple is a development of the primitive grave; and how can the theory of Buddhistic origin square with it? There is, however, a splendid way out of the difficulty. We are not able to trace the origin of the *vimâna* surmounting the temple from indigenous sources. It has a striking resemblance to the developed *stûpa,* and is also called by the name 'stûpi.' Therefore, it is "nothing more or less than a conventionalized model of a mediaeval Buddhist *stûpa*, erected purely as an architectural ornament, denoting the position of the image enshrined within the building."[5] Thus the one feature of the Dravidian temple which defied explanation from native sources appears to have been sufficiently accounted for, and the difficult problem concerning its origin seems to have been finally solved.

[1] Annual Report of the Archæological Department, Southern Circle, 1915–16, p. 30.

[2] Ibid., p. 30.

[3] Ibid., p. 31.

[4] Ibid., p. 31.

[5] Ibid., p. 31.

CHAPTER VIII

THE BUDDHIST ORIGIN OF THE HINDU TEMPLE

The theory, which has been stated in the last chapter, is evidently ingenious; and at first sight, there does not seem to be any cogent reason for us to disagree with it. It is a favourite dogma with a class of writers to deny the existence of sculpture and architecture in India before the advent of Buddhism. According to them the Mauryas were the first to introduce stone architecture in India. Judging, however, from the few models of sculpture and architecture of the period that still exist, we have reason to conclude that the Mauryan stone-masons were masters in their art, and not copyists of wooden models in stone. It would have required, at least several hundreds of years before the Indian sculpture and architecture could have reached that stage of development which it did during the time of the Mauryas. This is, however, a very wide question and it is not possible to discuss it here at length.

Apart from the discussion of the origins of Hindu architecture, it is easy to establish the priority of the Hindu temple to the Buddhist *stûpa* from literature both Buddhistic and Brahmanic.

The Buddhist divine Nâgasêna who lived in the first century before Christ bears testimony to the existence of Hindu temples in his time. In his *Miḷinda-Pañha,* he enumerates eight places which a contemplative Buddhist should avoid:

> "Uneven ground, unsafe, and windy spots
> And hiding places, and *god-haunted shrines,*
> High roads and bridges, and all bathing ghats—
> These eight places avoid, when talking of high things." [1]

The 'god-haunted shrines' must necessarily refer to the Hindu temples; for it is difficult to imagine how a pious Buddhist divine like Nâgasêna could have described the Buddhist shrines as 'god-haunted.'

Again, the Buddhist *suttas* very often refer to 'shrines,' which appear to be a common feature of the religions of the

Gangetic valley. Most of them, however, are chaityas which are pre-Buddhistic in origin. We shall have to discuss this topic separately in a different context. For the present, it is enough to note that the *Brahmajâla-Sutta* enumerates the worship of a number of deities whom the Buddha condemns. It refers especially to the worship of 'The Fire,' 'The Sun' and 'The Great One.' The goddess of Luck, Siri, appears to have received her own share of popular devotion; but the *suttas* do not tell us whether these deities were worshipped in temples. The *Ambaṭṭa-Sutta*, however, tells us definitely that, at least, one of them, Agni, was worshipped in a temple.

> "And now Ambaṭṭa," says the Buddha, "in case any recluse or Brahman, without having thoroughly attained unto this supreme perfection, in wisdom and conduct, and without having attained to living only on fruits, fallen of themselves, and without having attained to living only on bulbs and roots and fruits, *should build himself a fire-shrine* near the boundaries of some village, or some town, and there dwell serving the fire-god, then verily he turns out worthy only to be a servant unto him that hath attained to wisdom and righteousness." [2]

It is probable that the other deities whose worship was condemned by the Buddha should have received similar attention from their devotees. This view is strongly supported by the evidence of the so-called Brahmanic literature. The *Manu-Smṛiti* and the Epics contain many references to temples. But they are not generally taken into account. The *Râmâyaṇa* describes temples built in a highly ornate style; but we cannot take them into consideration, because the *Râmâyaṇa* is said to be a comparatively recent work. According to Hopkins the earliest Bhârata makes mention of *dêvatâyatanas* or the temples; but he destroys the usefulness of his remark for our purpose by observing that they were insignificant from an architectural point of view.[3] We are, therefore, obliged to draw our information from other sources. We begin, then, with Megasthenes whose veracity appears to be unimpeachable.

> "In their collective capacity," says he in his *Indika*, "they have charge both of their special departments and also of matters affecting general interest, as the keeping of public buildings in proper repair, the regulation of prices, the care of markets, harbours, and *temples*." [4]

This passage is the 'sheet-anchor' of the chronology of our temples. They were so many about 320 B.C., that they demanded the attention of the imperial government of the Mauryas. The Greek ambassador's reference to temples is borne out by the evidence of Indian writers.* The *Arthaśâstra* of Kauṭilya, the Chancellor of Chandragupta Maurya, although a book on politics, throws a flood of light on the social and religious conditions of Northern India of the 4th century B.C. It mentions *chaityas* and temples which appear to have been very common all over the country. The *chaitya* had not yet become exclusively Buddhistic. It was still a popular institution common to the men of all sects. Demons and evil spirits were the deities presiding over it. They would get angry, and cause national calamities, unless they were satisfied by the sacrifice of animals such as he-goats.

Temples were numerous, and they were dedicated to gods of all sects. The Vedic gods like Varuṇa and the Aśvins, the Purâṇic deities like Śiva and Kumâra, the Jaina deities like Aparâjita, and the popular deities like Vaiśravaṇa and Madirā had all their temples. The cowherds living in their ranches, worshipped their own god Samkarshaṇa. Besides the Nâga deities claimed their own share of popular devotion. In the cities as well as in the country, on the public roads and at the sacred *tirthas*, temples were built, and gods and goddesses were worshipped. Kauṭilya agrees with Megasthenes in telling us that the temples were under the control of the government. A special department to govern the religious institutions, was in existence. The head of this department was called the Superintendent of Religious Institutions. (Bk. V. 2.). Kauṭilya gives us a mass of information regarding the temples. Although the *Arthaśâstra* does not describe anywhere a temple, it throws out here and there valuable hints which tell us that the temple was a structural building. We have in Bk. II. 3 a description of the temple of Kumârī, the goddess of war. Its external area was "one-and-a-half times" that of its innermost room, "a circular building with an arch-way." Bk. XI. 1. mentions the gates of temples (*chaityadaivata dvâra rakshasthâna*); and Bk. XII. 5 gives us more particulars:

"A wall or stone, kept by mechanical contrivance, may by loosening the fastenings, be let to fall on the head of the enemy, when he has entered

---

* The Ghosundi stone inscription (*Ep. Ind. XVI*, p. 25) shows that temples of Hindu gods existed in Northern India in the time of the Sungas. Mr. K. P. Jayaswal, the learned editor of the inscription says,—"It is the earliest monumental proof of the fact that temples were erected to Vâsudêva and to his brother, and that the followers of the cult included even Brahmins"—"The age of the inscription can be assigned between circa 200 B.C., and 150 B.C."

into a temple; stones and weapons may be showered over his head from the topmost storey *uttamāgara*; or a door panel may be let to fall; or a huge rod kept over a wall or partly attached to a wall may be made to fall over him."

We understand from the above that the temple was a structural building with gateways and doors; it contained an inner room (the sanctum), and an outer room surrounding it. What is more important, it was a building consisting of several storeys. One is tempted to think that Kauṭilya refers to a temple-*vimâna* in the above passage (XII. 5). There is nothing improbable in such an idea. According to *Mânasâra*, a temple "*vimâna* consists of from one to twelve storeys."[5] Several temples containing three or four storeys exist even at the present day. Moreover, the *vimânas* were quite familiar to the people of India during the time of the Mauryas. The Aśôkan inscriptions mention them, not in connection with the temples, but in connection with the aerial cars (*vimânas*) of the gods. The Girnar Rock Edict has

विमानदर्सणा च हस्तिदर्सणा च अगिखंधानि च दिव्यानि रूपानि दसयित्पा जनं[6] (*Vimâna-darsaṇâ cha hasti-darsaṇâ cha agikhamdhâni cha divyâni rûpâni dasayitpâ janam*).

Now, the temple-*vimâna* is very closely akin to the *vimânas* of the gods. The *Râmâyaṇa*, Bk. I) compares the upper parts of the palaces in Ayōdhyā to the *vimâṇas* of the Siddhas, a species of gods.

Vimânaṁ iva siddhânâṁ tâpasâdhigataṁ divi
Sunivêsita vêśmântâm, etc.[7]

(The upper parts of the palaces were like the *vimânas* of the Siddhas which were brought down by the power of *tapas* to the earth.)

In another place, the city is described as,
Sarva-ratna-sāmâkirnâṁ vimâna-gṛha-śobhitâm.[8]

The houses in Ayōdhyâ had *vimânas*, and there is nothing extraordinary about this; for the *Mânasâra* tells us "that the *vimâna* which is a special feature of the temple construction is permissible in palaces, where it can be raised either over the main entrance-way to the palace or over the Durbar hall, or even over the *pûjâgriha* of the king, specially built for the worship of his *kuladêvata* or the deity of the royal household."[9] There is mention of the *vimâna* also with reference to the buildings of Brahmanas and Vaiśyas.*

We are justified in concluding, on the authority of the *Rāmāyaṇa* that the *vimânas* of the temples and the *vimânas* of the gods are similar in form. The *vimânas* of the Aśôkan inscriptions must have resembled the *vimânas* of more substantial buildings. Therefore, the suggestion that Kauṭilya seems to refer to a temple with a *vimāna* in Bk. XXII. 5 is not altogether improbable.

The inmost shrine of the temple contained the idol made of stone representing the deity. Images of Varuṇa, Nâgas, Yakshas, and goddesses were regularly worshipped. Articles of worship were brought into the city from outside (II. 21); "flowers and fruits" were used in the worship (II. 24); "auspicious hymns" were chanted during the service (II. 3); gifts were given on such occasions (II. 3); Devadâsis attended "the temple on service" (II. 23); on festival occasions, the gods were taken out in processions (XII. 3), which perhaps followed fixed routes in cities. II. 3 mentions the *dêvapatham*, 'the road for the gods.' The temples appear to have had cars attached to them. II. 33 describes various types of chariots which the Superintendent of chariots should get constructed. One of them is the *dêvaratha*, 'the chariot of gods.' Bulls were 'let out' in honour of gods, and any one found riding on them was punished (III. 13). Sufficient provision was also made for the rehabilitation of ruined temples. They like the other religious buildings were repaired, in the absence of claimants, either by the villagers or charitable people (III. 10). The temple of the 4th century B.C. appears to have been more or less the same kind of building as the later Hindu temple. But it was not invented by the Indians of that age. There is some evidence to show that the temple was known much earlier than the 4th century B. C. Pâṇini, the ancient Śânskṛit grammarian, who is said to have lived in the time of the Nandas, refers in V. 3, 96 and 97, of his *Ashṭâdhyâyî* to two classes of images. These *sûtras* and the commentaries thereon formed the subject of a learned discussion by Sten Konow in the *Indian*

---

* The *vimânas* of the royal palaces at Vijayanagar, Penukoṇḍa and Chandragiri may be taken as illustrations of the statement of the *Mānasara*.

Antiquary, Vol. XXXVIII. He establishes the fact that the images of the Hindu gods such as Vâsudêva, Ŝiva, Skanda, etc. were worshipped at the time of Pâṇini and Patañjali. It is not very unreasonable to suppose that temples also existed with the images of gods that were the objects of popular worship. Such a view gains strength from the evidence that is drawn from other sources. The Gautama *Dharma-śâstra* is said to be "the oldest of the existing works on the sacred law."[10] It is older than Baudhâyana and Âpastamba, and may very well have been anterior to Pâṇini. This book mentions 'images of gods' and temples.

The reference to images of gods occurs in IX,—

12. "Facing or within sight of wind, fire, Brahmanas, the sun, water, (*the image of the*) *gods*, and cows, he shall not eject urine, or fæces, or other impurities."

13. "He shall not stretch out his feet towards those divine beings." (S.B.E., Vol. II, p. 220).

The reference to temples occurs in IX.—

66 "He shall pass excellent (beings and things), auspicious (beings), *temples of gods*, cross-roads and the like with his right hand towards them." Ibid, p. 226

V. 14. mentions '*Parishkandha*' (translated as temple of gods) as one of the places which destroys sins; but we are not quite certain about the meaning of *Parishkandha*.

Temples were known to Gautama, and he enjoins that a Brahman who had received the 'forty' important sacraments should reverence them. Gautama is certainly a more ancient authority than Kauṭilya, and his book perhaps takes us to the days of the Buddha himself.

It has been made clear by the foregoing references that the Hindu temple existed as early as the time of the Buddha. Perhaps, it was originally a Dravidian institution, which the Aryan conquerors had, in course of ages, incorporated into their faith; for recent excavations in the Punjab and Sind show that the temple was a familiar institution in the 3rd millennium before Christ. "The temples," says Sir John Marshall, "stand on elevated ground, and are distinguished by the relative smallness of their chambers, and the exceptional thickness of their walls—

a feature which suggests that they were several storeys in height." [11]

References :—

[1] Sacred Books of the East, Vol. XXXV.
[2] Dialogues of the Buddha, Vol. 1.
[3] Hopkins: Epic Mythology.
[4] MacCrindle: Magasthenes' Indika Fr. XXXIV.
[5] Ram Raz., p. 48.
[6] The Corpus Inscriptionum Indicarum, Vol. I (revised edition) pp. 7–8.
[7] Râmâyaṇa, Bk. I.
[8] Ibid.
[9] Ananthāḻwar: The Indian Architecture, Vol. I, p. 240.
[10] Geo. Buhler: Introduction to Gautama Dharmaśâstra, S.B.E., Vol. II.
[11] Sir John Marshall: "The Times," Feb. 1926.

CHAPTER IX

THE EXTENT OF THE BUDDHIST INDEBTEDNESS

i. The Stupa

It has been pointed out in the last chapter that the Hindu temple existed at the time, when the Buddha was preaching his new religion to the people of the Gangetic valley. If it is admitted that the Hindu temple existed as early as the 6th century before Christ, the theory which traces its origin to the Buddhist *stūpa* cannot be maintained. Still, we have to account for the extraordinary resemblance between the developed Buddhist *stūpa* and the Hindu temple. We can give a very satisfactory explanation of this resemblance by assuming that the Hindu temple served as a model for the Buddhists to build a shrine to their own deity, when they felt the need of a temple. The Hindus did not borrow their temples, as it is generally supposed, from the Buddhists; but, in fact, they taught the Buddhists the art of *stūpa*-building. The Buddhists were the real borrowers in this as in many other cases.

The Buddha in organizing his new religion borrowed freely from the social and political institutions of his time. We shall consider some of them here. Since the time of the Buddha the terms *Sramaṇa* and *bikshu* were applied to the Buddhist monks. They are generally supposed to be words specially associated with Buddhism ; but on a closer examination of ancient Sānskṛit literature, it is found that they were known even before the birth of the Buddha and used to denote ascetics who had abandoned the world and adopted a wandering life. The 'Śramaṇas' did not belong to any one community in particular. All who did not recognize the Brāhmanic religion, and adopting a wandering life, devoted their time to the pursuits of truth were called by that name. They were not popular among the orthodox ; hence they were occasionally persecuted.

At the time of the Buddha, they were considered equal to the Brāhmaṇas ; hence the oft-repeated phrase 'Brāhmaṇas and Śramaṇas.' The Buddha himself was generally known as

'Śramaṇa Gôtama.' This indicates the existence of Śramaṇas other than Gôtama. He was called a Śramaṇa because he possessed many of the characteristics of a Śramaṇa. The *Brahma-jâla-Sutta* mentions a large number of Śramaṇas with whom the Buddha disagreed. The term 'Śramaṇa' was in common use before the time of the Buddha. After the death of its founder, Buddhism became so very popular that it absorbed all the Śramaṇas. Consequently the term Śramaṇa came to mean, in course of time, 'a monk who accepted the teachings of the Buddha.'

The word '*bhikku*' which the Buddha uses invariably in addressing his followers, is also used by Gautama in his *Dharma-Sūtras* to denote a man in the third *āśrama*. In the later law-books, '*parivrājaka*' and '*vānaprastha*' take its place. We understand from this that at the time of Gautama and of some early law-givers, there were Brahman and perhaps other non-Brahman *bhikshus*, and that the Buddha was only using a current word in addressing his disciples.

It is not only the terms like '*Sramaṇa*' and '*Bhikku*' which the Buddha borrowed from the Brahmans, but he appears to have incorporated the code of discipline of Brahman monks into his system. His *Vinaya* appears to have been based upon an earlier Vinaya. The word '*vinaya*' itself was drawn from Hindu sources; for we find Kauṭilya designating the first book of his *Arthaśāstra* as *Vinayādhikārikam*, 'Concerning Discipline.' The dress and the regulations regarding diet and habitation appear to have been modelled upon corresponding rules, *e.g.*, rules of the *Dharma-śâstras* in the Brahmanic system.[1] Buhler in his translation of the Gautama *Dharma-sâstra* expresses the opinion that the "'Vasso' of the Bauddhas and Jainas is also derived from a Brahmanical source."[2] Moreover, it has been recently shown by Mr. K. P. Jayaswal that both the Buddha and Mahâvîra organised their respective churches on the basis of some of the republican constitutions of their time.[3]

The worship of trees and serpents, Yakshas and other demons was, as already pointed out, a feature of the pre-Buddhistic Hindu religion. It was also adopted by the Buddhists so thoroughly that it came to be looked upon as a specially Buddhistic institution. These may, however, be set aside as instances of unimportant indebtedness; but the same thing cannot be said of the two examples of borrowing which are described below.

One of them is the '*Stûpa*.' It is generally admitted that the *stûpa* was a pre-Buddhistic institution which was introduced into the new faith by the master himself. So much is implied by a passage of the *Mahâparinibbâṇa-Sutta*.[3] Its testimony is corroborated by the discovery of some *stûpas* belonging to certain communities other than the Buddhistic. A few years ago, a Jaina *stûpa* was discovered at Mathura.[4] More recently still, another belonging to the Brahmans was brought to light at Lauriya-Nandanghar by Dr. Bloch of the Archæological Department. The clay mounds with the wooden pillars [5] having a deposit of bones on their tops claim their relationship with the spherical *stûpa* with its 'tee' and casket of relics.

The funeral customs of some South Indian communities which Mr. Thurston describes in his *Castes and Tribes* throw some fresh light on the origin of the *stûpa*. The *stûpa* is still associated with the burial or cremation ceremonies of these people; and it presents certain interesting features which dispel some misconceptions which are current about its origin. The modern South Indian *stûpa* is associated with a tree on the one hand, and a funeral car which resembles the Buddhist 'tee' with its tiers of umbrellas on the other. The following extracts from Thurston give us an idea of the funeral customs referred to.

The Billavas of South Canara usually burn their dead, 'though in some cases, burial is resorted to.' The ashes when collected are 'buried on the spot.' "If the body has been buried, a straw figure is made, and burnt over the grave, and the ashes are buried there. A small conical mound called dhûpé is made, and a *tulasi* plant is stuck in it . . . On the thirteenth day, the final death ceremonies or bojja are performed. On the evening of the previous day, four poles for the construction of the Upparige or gudikattu (car) are planted round the dhûpé. At the house, on or near the place where the deceased breathed his last, a small bamboo car in three tiers is constructed and decorated with coloured cloths. This car is called Nirneralu. A lamp is suspended from the car, and a cot is placed on the ground beneath it, and the jewels and clothes of the dead person are laid thereon. On the following morning, the Upparige is constructed with the assistance of the caste barber . . . . The various articles are collected in a bundle, which is placed in a palanquin, and carried in procession by two men to the Upparige which has been constructed over the dhûpé . . . . . Those present go thrice round the Upparige, and the chief mourner unties the bundle and places its contents on the car . . . . All present then leave the spot, and the barber removes the cloths from the car, and pulls it down. Sometimes, if the dead person happens to be an important member of the community a small car is constructed, and taken in procession round the Upparige . . . . "[6]

The first point that we have to notice in this passage is the 'small conical mound called dhûpé.' Now, it is obvious that the word 'dhûpé' is the corrupted form of Skt. 'Stûpa,' the well-known ancient Hindu institution. The next point of interest is the tulasi plant which is stuck in the dhûpé. This again brings to our mind the ancient custom of planting trees over the graves. In this connection we may also note a custom prevalent among the Bottadas, a class of Uriya cultivators and labourers, who plant a banyan or pipal tree on the place where the corpse is cremated.[7] Moreover, the close association of the tree with the *stûpas* gives us an insight into the probable origin of umbrellas over the Buddhist *stûpas*. Lastly, the custom of constructing the *upparige* or *guḍikaṭṭu* must also be noted. The meanings of these words are very suggestive. *Upparige* means 'a building with an upper storey'; *guḍikaṭṭu* is a compound word consisting of two words *guḍi* meaning 'a temple' and *kaṭṭu* meaning 'to build'; thus the whole word means 'temple-building.' We understand from this that the building constructed over the *dhûpé* contains at least two storeys and it is regarded as a temple. This, perhaps, throws a hint about the origin of the temple; but it is regrettable that the description of the 'Upparige' is not given; probably it resembles the 'nirneralu' which is said to be built in three tiers. It is, perhaps, the same kind of structure built on such occasions by the Bants. Some days after the cremation of a Bant, "a barber, a washerman, and a carpenter build upon the spot where the corpse was burnt a lofty structure made of bamboo and areca palm in an odd number of tiers supported by an odd number of posts. It is decorated with cloths, fruits, tender cocoanuts, sugar cane, flowers, mango leaves, areca-palm flowers, &c., and a fence is set up around it."[8] The Masadika Bants follow the same custom. "The lofty structure called Gurige or Upparige is set up over the dhûpé or the ashes heaped up into a mound, or in the field in which the body is cremated, only in the event of deceased being a person of importance. In some places two kinds of structures are used, one called Gurige composed of several tiers for males, and the other called dela gûḍu, consisting of a single tier for females."

This passage makes it clear that the *upparige* is composed of several tiers, and it is built over the *dhûpé*. Moveover, a fence is also said to be set up around it. Here we seem to stumble against the prototype of the Buddhistic *stûpa*. The *dhûpé* corresponds to the *stûpa*, the fence which is set up around it to the elaborately carved stone railings seen around early the Buddhist *stûpas*; and the *upparige* which is the conventionalised form of the original tree, to the 'tee' and the umbrellas. The *dhûpe*, the *upparige*, and the fence do not exhibit any trace of Buddhism. They are distinctly non-Buddhistic in origin. This is clearly shown by their association with the funeral car, which is akin to the huge cars that are attached to our temples.

What is said above is enough to show that the *stûpa* was, at one time, an institution common to all Indians. Although the Buddhists brought it to such prominence as to make it appear pre-eminently their own, it still lurks in obscure corners of Hinduism, where it has not yet lost its original character.

References :—

1	Gautama Dharma Sutras ...	...	Buhler, S. B. E., Vol. II, pp. 193–4.
2	The Hindu Polity ...	...	K. P. Jayaswal.
3	The Dialogues of the Buddha, Vol. II.		Rhys David.
4	Do.		Do.
5	The Arch. Sur. Ind. 1906-7	...	...
6	The Castes and Tribes, Vol. I	...	E. Thurston.
7	Do.	...	Do.
8	Do.	...	Do.

A Chaitya

From Havell's *Indian Architecture.*

CHAPTER X

THE EXTENT OF THE BUDDHIST INDEBTEDNESS

ii. The Chaitya

Another institution which has been considered specially Buddhistic is the chaitya. The word '*chaitya*' is generally derived from *chiti* or 'funeral pyre'; but it is not clear how exactly it is connected with *chiti*. The epics appear to throw some light on the problem. Both the *Râmâyaṇa* and the *Mahâbhârata* mention *chaityas* in several places. The *Mahâbhârata* gives us some idea of what may be regarded as the earliest history of the chaitya. Originally the *chaitya* is not a building, religious or otherwise, but a tree. Thus in Bk. XII. 59, we have, "He should also cut down all the smaller trees excepting those trees called *chaityas*;" 'he should not touch (its) very leaves."[1] The Vana-Parvan also refers to 'sacred trees.'

According to Bk. XII. 69. 41. &c., "gods, yakshâs, râkshasas, nâgas, piśâchas, serpents, gandharvas, apsarasas, and cruel bhûtas dwell in the chaityas." Again, Bk. III. 125. 17, mentions "chaityas of the Three-and-thirty (gods)." The *chaitya*, therefore, in the *Mahâbhârata*, is a tree in which spirits good or evil are supposed to live. What then has this tree to do with 'chiti' or the funeral pyre from which the word 'chaitya' is derived? It is not possible to give a definite answer to this question. We can establish the connection between the tree and the funeral pyre in a way. The clue is suggested by the *Mahâbhârata*, XIII, 141. 18: The crematorium is said to be generally shaded "by the branches of the banyan (tree)." In Bk. IV, the cemetery outside the capital of King Virâṭa is called *pitṛivana* or 'the grove of the fathers.' Therefore, the chief characteristic of the cemetery in the *Mahâbhârata* appears to be the presence of big trees. Their presence in the crematorium can be accounted for by assuming that people were accustomed to plant them on the graves. The Ṛig-Vêda (X. 58. 7; 16, 3)[1] expresses a belief among the Āryans that "the spirits of the dead enter plants and trees." It was, perhaps, due to a belief of this kind that the Āryans planted trees upon the graves. The vestiges of this custom can be seen in the obscure allusions to "the pillar" of R.V., X. 18,[3] and in the Vaidica graves at Lauriya-Nandangar. This also explains why the *Mahâbhârata*, (XII, 69. 41), declares that the *chaityas* "are the resorts of gods, yakshas, rākshasas, etc."

It is obvious from this, that the 'chaitya' in the *Mahâbhârata* is a tree, planted originally on the grave, and after the introduction of cremation, upon the place where the body was cremated. Therefore, the tree that was planted on the *chiti* became the *chaitya*. It was considered worthy of worship, because it was the abode generally of evil spirits.

The *Râmâyaṇa* represents a later stage in the development of the *chaitya*. Here, it is no longer a tree, but a shrine or a temple. The *Râmâyaṇa* refers to a *chaitya* in the crematorium :

'*śmaśâna chaitya pratimô bhûshitô 'pi bhayankaraḥ.*'

Sundarakāṇḍa, ch. 22 : 29.

R. 5. 15 describes the *chaitya-prâsâda* of Râvaṇa. The *chaitya-prâsâda* is a royal palace built by Râvaṇa in his pleasure garden, Aśôka, on the model probably of a *chaitya*. "It is described as having *vêdikas*, terraces, coral stairs, a thousand pillars and a high roof."[4] If we are right in assuming that the *chaitya-prâsâda* was modelled on the *chaitya*, a shrine seems to have grown up, in course of time, around the sacred tree, and to have claimed equal honour with the temple.

The worship of the tree certainly represents an earlier phase of religion than that of the shrine. This is a fact familiar to many Indians. Tree-worship was unknown to the Vedic religion ; but it plays, even at the present day, a very important part in the religious life of the Dravidian South. It is inferred from this that tree-worship has been very early borrowed by the Āryans from the non-Āryan Dravidians of India. During the epic age it became an important part of the Hindu religion. The combined evidence of the two epics shows that the *chaitya* was originally a Hindu institution. The same fact is clearly indicated by the Buddhist *suttas* also. The *Mahâparinibhâṇa Sutta* alludes to them as a general feature of the religious life of that time. The Buddha declares, on one occasion, while speaking of the people of Vaiśâli that, "so long as they honour and esteem and revere and support the Vajjian shrines (*chêtiyâni*) in town or country, and allow not the proper offerings and rites, formerly given and performed, to fall into desuetude . . . . ," [5] they shall prosper.

On another occasion, he enumerates all the *chaityas* at Vaiśâli.

"When I was once staying, O Brahman, at Vêsâli at Sârandada Shrine, I taught the Vajjians these conditions of welfare." [6]

"So the Exalted One proceeded to Châpala Shrine, and when he had come down on the mat spread out for him, and the venerable Ânanda took his seat respectfully beside him. Then the Exalted One addressed Ânanda and said,—'How delightful a spot Ânanda is Vêsâli and how charming is the Udêna Shrine, and the Gotamaka Shrine and the shrine of the Seven Mangoes, and the shrine of the Many Sons, and the Sârandada Shrine, and the Châpala Shrine." [7]

According to the *Sumangaḷa Vilâsini* quoted in the Dialogues, these were 'Yekkha-cêtiyâni', *i.e., chaityas* dedicated to the *yakshas*. They were, as Rhys Davids remarks, "shrines of pre-Buddhistic worship."[8] They did not become exclusively Buddhistic even in the fourth century before Christ.

The *Arthaśâstra* of Kauṭilya teems with allusions to *chaityas*. It appears that the *chaitya* was still a Hindu institution. Certain interesting details regarding the *chaitya* are given in one place. "On full and new moon days, the worship of the *chaityas* may be performed by placing on a verandah, offerings such as an umbrella, the picture of an arm, a flag, and a he-goat."[9]

This was done in order to propitiate the demons which were supposed to cause national calamities. The first observation that we have to make in this connection is that the *chaitya* is a building with a verandah; next, that *chchâga* (he-goat) and *hasta* (hand) are included among the offerings. Whatever may be the meaning of 'hasta,' we need not have any doubt regarding that of 'chchâga.' It refers to the sacrifice of a he-goat. This is really interesting. The he-goat, especially, the black he-goat, is the most valuable victim that can be offered to a village deity in South India. These considerations justify us in concluding that the *chaitya* was originally a Hindu institution, before it was appropriated by the Buddhists.

The foregoing discussion has shown that the Buddhists borrowed a good many things from the Hindus, in giving a definite shape to their religion. The extent of their indebtedness is not limited to the borrowing of a few technical terms and points of discipline; it extends to the incorporation of the *stûpa* and the *chaitya* which are the central features of practical Buddhism.

References :—

1	Mahābhārata	...	Pratāpa Chandra Roy's translation.
2	Rig-Vēda ..		Griffith's translation, Vol. IV.
3	Ibid. ...		Ibid.
4	W. Hopkins		The Epic Mythology.
5	Rhys Davids		The Dialogues of the Buddha, Vol. II, p. 80.
6	Ibid. ...		Ibid.
7	Ibid. ...	...	Ibid., p. 110.
8	Rhys Davids	...	Dialogues, Vol. II, footnote to p. 110.
9	Kauṭilīya Arthaśāstra		Shama Sastri's translation, p. 256.

CHAPTER XI

THE HINDU TEMPLE AND THE BUDDHIST TEMPLE

We have shown that the Hindu temple existed almost from the time of the Buddha, and that the *stûpa* and the *chaitya*, the two institutions which the Buddhists regarded as the exclusive features of their religion were borrowed from the Hindus. If then, in course of time, one of them, the *stûpa*, showed a tendency to become a tower, it is not unreasonable to suppose that it was due to the influence which the temple should have exercised upon it. In other words, the Buddhist temple of the early Middle Ages, as we shall soon realise, was the result of the influence exercised upon the *stûpa* by the Hindu temple of an earlier day.

The religion of the Buddha differed from Brahmanism in its denial of god. The Buddha allowed, it is true, room for the earlier gods to remain in his religion; but, in admitting them, he reduced them to the position of mortals, a kind of supermen. They were as much subject to birth, growth, and decay, and as much immersed in the ocean of *samsâra* as men themselves. They had to work out their salvation in the same way as men were expected to do. They lost, therefore, much of their value and importance in the estimation of men. The ultimate goal which the Buddha taught his disciples to strive after was Nirvâṇa. It was the desire of every Buddhist to attain Nirvâṇa, and thereby put an end to the unending series of births and deaths. Consequently, the New Religion did not require either temples or idols. We do not hear much of them in the Buddhist *Suttas*, except on rare occasions when they are introduced into the canon only to be condemned by the Buddha. But from the very early days of Buddhism, there was one institution which took the place of the temple in the community of the faithful. This was the sacred *stûpa* which might be said to have almost received the sanction of the master. As a funeral monument of a saint or a great man, it had already become the object of popular worship. As the Buddha had on one occasion expressed a desire that a *stûpa* might be erected on his grave, the disciples believed that he had sanctioned its worship. When he died, *stûpas* were built over his remains, and became the objects of constant and regular worship. This was enough to satisfy the disciples, and especially as most of them had known the master, they did not feel the need of offering worship to any other visible representation.

At the time of the death of the Buddha, the disciples were only a handful. They were generally drawn from the upper classes of society. Most of them were very well educated, and could appreciate the new doctrines. Their importance as a community, however, was not very great. They were, as Dr. V. A. Smith observes, a mere 'local sect' until the time of the emperor Aśōka. Further, as he adds, "The personal ministry of Gautama Buddha was confined to a comparatively small area . . . between Gaya, Allahâbâd, and the Himâlaya . . . When he died about 487 B.C., Buddhism was merely a sect of Hinduism, unknown beyond very restricted limits . . . ."[1]

The new faith as originally preached, was satisfactory, as we have already remarked, to the disciples within this limited area. But Buddhism unlike Brahmanism was a proselytizing religion, and the ambition of the early Buddhists was to make it the universal religion of India. The tenets which were originally formed to satisfy the spiritual needs of a few, confined to a limited area, were required to satisfy the needs of millions of men all over the length and the breadth of a whole continent. The religions of the new converts were not always the same as those of the old disciples. Therefore, when the propagators of the new religion went abroad to preach, they were obliged to modify the doctrine to suit the new conditions, make room for some new sects, and admit certain alien institutions into their religion. Fortunately, much information regarding the religious conditions of the times is available to us.

In the days of Pâṇini, the worship of images appears to have already become popular. According to the old scholia referred to by Konow, the images mentioned by Pâṇini were those of Vâsudêva, Śiva, Skanda, Vishṇu, and Âditya,—members all of the Purâṇic Hindu pantheon. Patañjali, who is said to have been a contemporary of Pushyamitra, supplies us with some interesting information on this point. He tells us that the images mentioned by Pâṇiṇi were used "for immediate worship"; further that "the Mauryas had images made from greed." From the discussions of grammarians, we understand that image-worship was very popular, and that the images, in all cases, were those of the Hindu gods.

It is, however, to Kauṭilya, a contemporary of Chandragupta Maurya, that we are very heavily indebted for giving us a vivid picture of the religious conditions of India in the 4th century B.C. His *Arthaśâstra* mentions some of the important religious sects of his time. Besides the Hindus, there were the Âjîvakas and the Buddhists. Monks and nuns, and Pâshanḍas, an indefinite class of heretics, could be seen everywhere in the country. People believed in and practised magic extensively. Animals were sacrificed on a large scale, especially by the Brahmanas in their forest hermitages. The country was full of *tîrthas* and sacred places, which pious pilgrims constantly visited. Trees were considered holy; hence they became the objects of pious popular devotion. Yakshas and nâgas, so very prominent in later Buddhism had already become popular; greater honour was paid to them than even to the gods. The worship of the *chaityas* was a common feature of religious life. The Buddhists were not prominent, and the *stûpa* is mentioned only once.

Such was the religious condition of the society into which Buddhism was introduced. The professors of the new faith had to incorporate into it almost all the important elements of popular religion, in order to attain their object. The worship of images, chaityas, trees, Nâgas and Yakshas, magical practices, and pilgrimages were admitted, in course of time, into the new faith. Some of these were considered specially Buddhistic in later ages.*

Moreover, the reformed religion was profoundly influenced, very early in its career, by certain movements of thought. Brahmanism began to shed much of its formalism and put forth new shoots. The cult of Bhakti was gradually taking shape. Its influence is dimly discernible in the Upanishads. By the time of Pânini and Patanjali, Vâsudeva, the supreme god of the Bhâgavatas, had already become a powerful deity. The Bhakti-cult, however, finds its clearest expression in the *Bhagavadgîtâ*.

---

* The Buddha condemned most of these in the *Brahmajâla-Sutta*. See Dialogues, Vol. I.

1555—8

The most important feature of this new development of Brahmanism is its insistence on the worship of a personal god, who is the Lord of the universe. It had, therefore, a greater appeal to the human heart than Buddhism with its denial of god and assertion of impersonal Nirvâṇa as the ultimate reality. Hence it became a very serious rival for Buddhism to reckon with.

The desire to outrun the new rival, coupled with the natural craving of the heart to have some anthropomorphic form to worship, gave birth to a new form of Buddhism called Mahâyânism. A galaxy of saints was created, and Gautama, the Buddha, was deified. He now took the same place in his religion as Brahmā in Brahmanism. The Buddhists began to vie with the Hindus in building shrines intended for the habitation of their gods. At first, they were timid; they did not build temples resembling those of the Hindus, because the *stûpa* stood in their way. It had its origin in an earlier age when it was not intended to be a temple. And it had become the most sacred institution by the time when Mahâyâna was born. It was not possible either to abandon it completely or to modify its form radically. Nevertheless, the form of the *stûpa* gradually underwent a change. The original domical structure became, in course of time, conical in form, approximating itself more and more to the shape of the Hindu temple.

What has been said above is borne out by the *stûpas* that have come down to our own times. For the purpose of understanding the discussion, it is necessary that we should keep in mind the following fact:—The *stûpa* consists of two well defined parts, *viz.*, the dome, and the 'tee' surmounted by one or more umbrellas. "Both the domical *stûpa* and the 'tee' with the umbrellas became elongated in course of time, and assumed the shape of a temple."[3]

"The earliest *stûpas* were low in proportion to their diameter. Thus the oldest known example, that of Piprahwa (450 B. C.), stands only about 22 feet high, with a diameter at the base of 116 feet. As time went on the relative height increased. Thus the great *stûpa* at Sânchi erected some 200 years later, is about 54 feet high, while the diameter at the base of the dome is 106 feet. The proportional height here is just about half, whilst at Piprahwa, it is less than one-fifth. The Dhâmek Stûpa at Sâranâth near Benares, was erected several centuries later. Here the height is 110 feet above the surrounding ruins, and about 128 feet above the plain, with a diameter of only 93 feet. Thus the height is now considerably more than the diameter. In other words, the *stûpa* shows a tendency in course of time to assume the shape of a tower."[4] At Ajanta, "the low and almost bare hemisphere of the Asôkan age has become conventionalised into a tall ornamental tower surmounting an elaborately carved basement."[5]

The same development, or "elongation" as it is called, is also seen in the umbrellas.* The umbrella over the 'tee' was originally a tree with its foliage. It became conventionalised in

---

* Mr. Longhurst gives a fanciful account of the origin of the umbrellas over the *stûpas*. They did not originate, as he supposes, in the offering to a shrine of a royal umbrella by some imaginary pious monarch. It had, on the other hand, its root deep in the past. The so-called umbrella is the conventionalised tree planted upon the grave, or the one in whose foliage the bones of the dead were hidden. We have the traces of such a custom preserved both in our Vedic and Purâṇic literatures.

The funeral hymn RV. X. 18 mentions the pillar, which the *pitris* are required to hold firm; it also refers to 'the piled up earth' over the grave. Atharva Veda XVIII. 2. 34 refers to a different method of disposing of the dead:—

"They that are buried, they that are scattered (*vap*) away, they that are burned, and they that are set up (*uddhita*) etc."

Referring to the last, *uddhita*, Whitney says, "It evidently refers to exposure on something elevated, such as is practised by many people." (*Har. Or. Series*, Vol. 8). Perhaps, it alludes to the setting up of bones on the top of a pillar. The archaeological discoveries at Lauriya-Nandangar have thrown much light on these obscure allusions. Dr. Bloch found in some clay funeral mounds, long posts of sal wood with "a deposit of human bones and charcoal" on their top. These pillars seem to have taken the place of the tree upon the grave. It is said in RV. IX that Yama and Varuṇa, the two kings of the dead carouse in heaven with the *pitris* under the leafy foliage of a huge tree. The tree which was planted upon the graves might have been intended to symbolise the tree in heaven.

In the Mahâbhârata, bk. iv, the Pâṇḍavas hide their weapons on a tree in the cemetery outside the city of Virâṭa. In this connection the following passage occurs: "And Nakula ascended the tree and deposited on it the bows and other weapons. And he tied them first on those parts of the tree which would not break, and where the rain would not penetrate. And the Pâṇḍavas hung up a corpse (on the tree) knowing that people smelling the stench of the corpse would say—here sure is a dead body, and would avoid the tree from a distance. And on being asked by the shepherds and cowherds regarding the corpse, these repressers of foes said unto them: "This is our mother, aged one hundred and eighty years. We have hung up her dead body, in accordance with the custom observed by our forefathers."

This evidently refers to a custom of exposing the dead body on the trees which must have been familiar to the people at that time.

course of time; its origin was forgotten, and it was considered an umbrella. Fancy and excessive piety were responsible for the multiplication of its number, for instance, on some of the *stûpas* sculptured on the gateway of the great *stûpas* at Sânchi. Here the umbrellas are not arranged in tiers, but in various other ways; and at Amarâvati, they form a hat-like heap on the top of the 'tee.' At Ajanta, they assume the form of a steeple 'reaching almost the roof of the *chaitya*.'[6] Thus, at the beginning of the early Middle Ages, 'the bare hemisphere of Aśokan age' with its tee and umbrellas 'assumed the shape of a temple, square in plan, with a domed roof surmounted by an ornamental spire.'[7] The archaeological evidence that we have just considered points to some external influence which gradually transformed hemispherical *stûpa* into a conical or pyramidal tower. We believe that this external influence came from the side of the Hindu temple. The same set of facts, however, is generally advanced to show that the temple is a development of the *stûpa*. There are two objections which we have to raise against this position. In the first place, the Hindu temple, as we have already shown, was in existence at the time of Gautama, the law-giver in the 6th or 7th century before Christ. Therefore, it could not have been developed from the *stûpa*, which assumed a form analogous to the Hindu temple only in the 5th or the 6th century A. D. Secondly, the theory does not explain why a structure which had originally a low hemisphere as roof should have assumed the shape of a conical or a pyramidal tower. It is left to our imagination to picture the causes which were responsible for this development. If we agree that the Buddhists modelled the *stûpa* upon the temple, it becomes clear how a tower came out of an originally hemispherical structure.

References:—

[1] V. A. Smith ... The Early History of India, 3rd Edn., p. 188.
[2] Sten Konow ... The Indian Antiquary, Vol. XXXVIII, pp. 148–9.
[3] Longhurst ... Influence of Umbrella in Indian Art.
[4] do. ... Ibid.
[5] do. ... Ibid.
[6] do. ... Ibid.
[7] do. ... Ibid.

CHAPTER XII

THE PALLAVAS AND THE SOUTH INDIAN TEMPLE

The discussion has been carried so far, on general lines. It applies to the *vimânas* in general. Let us now examine its bearing on the South Indian type. The Dravidians are said to have borrowed it from the Buddhists for the purpose of adorning their temple with an ornamental headgear. At first sight, this seems to be a reasonable hypothesis, especially as there appears to be no other way of explaining its origin. If we closely examine it, we see at once that we are following a wrong track in accepting it, as the following discussion will show.

The beginning of the temple architecture in South India is attributed to the Pallavas who ruled the country during the 6th and 7th centuries A. D. Longhurst enunciates the current theory as follows: "The earliest Hindu temples in Southern India are those at Mahâbalipuram in the Chingleput district which are generally known as the 'Seven Pagodas.' The inscriptions on these temples record that they were hewn out of the living rock by the Pallavas in the 7th century A. D.; and the style of their architecture shows that they are stone models of former Buddhist buildings which have been adopted to suit the requirements of Hinduism."[1]

There are two facts which give to this theory some plausibility. In the first place, the total absence of any temple belonging to a date prior to the 7th century A.D.; and secondly, the construction of a large number of temples immediately after this period. These seem 'to lend weight to the surmise' that before this time, 'no temples were built'[2] in South India.

However, the Mandagapaṭṭu inscription of Mahêndravarman I, brought to light by the untiring zeal of the eminent Frenchman M. Jouveau Dubreuil has, in our opinion, overthrown the above theory. The inscription is a short one, and it runs as follows:—

एतदनिष्टकमद्रुमलो-
हमसुधं विचित्राचत्तेन
निर्म्मापितन्नृपेण ब्रह्मे
श्वरविष्णुलक्षितायतनम् ॥

'This is the temple caused to be constructed by the (king Vichitrachitta, for (*i.e.* to contain together the images of) Brahmâ, Îsvara, and Vishṇu, without (the use of) bricks, without timber, without metals, and without mortar.'[3]

'Vichitrachitta' is one of the many titles of Mahêndravarman I. According to this inscription, temples existed even before the time of Mahêndravarman I, only they were built of bricks, timber, metals and mortar. The inscription refutes the statement that Mahêndra was the first to introduce the art of temple-building into South India. We shall here consider the opinions of three of the most competent authorities on the subject :

Dubreuil says,—

"The Mandagapaṭṭu inscription clearly says that at the epoch of Mahêndra there existed also temples which were not cut in rocks, but which were built with brick, wood, metal, and mortar.

"The last inference is important . . . . The Mandagapaṭṭu inscription proves . . . that *the Hindus knew perfectly well how* to build temples. . . . Thus then at the epoch of Mahêndra, it is certain that there did exist temples of stone, brick, timber, metal and mortar, and that these buildings made of perishable materials have all fallen into ruins, and have been destroyed either by time or by men."[4]

Longhurst agrees with Dubreuil. He is of opinion that 'the curious-minded' was "the inventor or originator of the art of carving Hindu temples out of natural rock instead of building them in the usual way with bricks and lime, wooden pillars, and roofs decorated with metal finials."[5]

The same opinion is expressed more elaborately by Mr. Gopinatha Rao, the learned editor of the inscription. "The most important information conveyed by it is that before the time of Vichitrachitta, bricks, timber, metal, and mortar were the common building material. Evidently the basement and walls of buildings were of brick work plastered with chunam, and the superstructures were composed of wood-work, held in position by the use of metallic nails and bands. This, in fact, even to this day is the mode of construction on the Malabar coast . . . . The statement made in this inscription that Mahêndravarman did not employ bricks, timber, metal, and mortar clearly warrants our drawing the conclusion that temples built before his time, were all of such perishable materials as bricks, etc., they were all ruined in course of time, and that this is the first rock-cut shrine of his . . . . . . It is impossible for a number of temples to have come suddenly into existence, from the beginning of the 7th century, unless the building of the temples had been practised long before . . . ."[6]

The three writers whose views are quoted above express more or less an identical opinion on the subject. All the three agree in thinking that there were temples before the time of Mahêndravarman I and that they were built of mortar, brick, timber, etc. That timber was made use of in the construction of temples, especially of the *vimānas* is proved by the following reference in *Mânasâra*, a great work on architecture :

"*Vimānas*" according to it, "are of three sorts, distinguished from one another by the principal materials of which they are formed as *śuddha*, pure ; *miśra*, mixed ; and *sankîrṇa* or anomalous." (The materials used are, in the language of the Mandagapaṭṭu inscription 'timber, stone, brick, etc.') "An edifice is '*śuddha*' which is composed of but one material as stone, brick, etc., and this is considered best of all. '*Miśra*' is that which is composed of two kinds of material, such as brick and stone and metals ; and '*sankîrṇa*' is that which is a compound of three or more kinds of materials, as timber, stone, brick, metal, etc."[7]

There is also much epigraphical evidence which shows that temples existed in South India from very early times.

(1) The Tirukkaḷukunram grant of the Chola king Râjakêsarivarman tells us that a Pallava king called Skandasishya, a predecessor of Vâtâpikoṇḍa Narasimha-pôttarāiyar gave a certain land "free from taxes to the feet of the god of the holy Mûlasthâna (temple) at Tirukkaḷukunram." (*Ep. Ind.*, III, 277).

(2) The British Museum Plates of Chârudêvi, the queen of Yuva-mahârâja Buddhavarman, and the daughter-in-law of the Pallava king Vijaya-Skandavarman (*c.*A.D. 250–275) inform us that the queen made the grant of a field "to the god Nârâyaṇa of the Kuli-Mahatraka temple at Dâlûra." (*Ep. Ind.*, VIII, 143).

(3) The grants of the Śâlankâyana kings who ruled in Vengi from A.D. 250 to A.D. 450 allude to a temple of the Sun-god, Chitrarathasvâmi, at the city of Vengi (*Ep. Ind.*, IX, Jr. An. H. S. I).

(4) According to the Tâlaguṇḍa inscription of the Kadamba King Kakusthavarman, the Śiva temple at Sthânakundûra existed from the time of the Śâtakarni kings.

"Say-iha bhagavatô Bhavasyâdidêvasya sidhyâlaye . . . Sâtakarny-âdibhiś-śraddhayâ-abhyarchchitê &c." Here at the holy temple of the primeval god Bhava which was worshipped with faith by Śâtakarni and other kings, &c.

These extracts from old inscriptions clearly show that temples existed in all parts of South India from at least the second century of the Christian era.

Consequently, the theory that the Pallavas were the first to introduce temple-architecture in South India must be given up. What really the Pallavas had done for our temple is to substitute imperishable material such as stone for perishable materials like brick, timber, etc. in building temples.

Now, we have to ask the question, what was the form of the pre-Pallava temple? It is not very difficult to answer this question. The temples at Mahâbalipuram supply the necessary answer. As we have already noted, Mahêndravarman I introduced "the art of carving Hindu temples out of natural rock." In the Maṇḍagapaṭṭu inscription, he claims only the credit of substituting stone for more perishable building material. What he had actually done was to copy in 'natural rock' the brick and timber models of his time. He built rock temples at Mahâbalipuram on the pattern of pre-existing brick and timber temples. "The most casual visitor," says Longhurst, "to the wonderful Pallava monuments at the Seven Pagodas must have noticed that all the monolithic free-standing temples, locally known as 'rathas' are obviously only stone models of buildings constructed with brick and mortar with timber-framed roofs decorated with copper-gilt ornaments like those referred to in the inscription quoted above."

There is also another source from which we can have an idea of the shape of the pre-Pallava temple. This is the huge wooden pyramidal car which is usually attached to all our temples. The temple cars, it must be remembered, are called *rathas*, 'cars'; it is by this term that the monolithic temples at Mahâbalipuram are generally known. The term *vimâna* also means a 'moving car.' There seems to be some sort of connection, between 'ratha' and 'vimâna.' Dr. A. K. Coomāraswāmi makes a pointed reference to this resemblance. "The resemblance of the Âryâvarta *śikhara* to the bamboo scaffolding of a processional car is too striking to be accidental. More than that, we actually find stone temples of great size provided with enormous stone wheels (Konarâk, Vijayanagar): and the monolithic temples at Mahâbalipuram are actually called *rathas*, that is, cars, while the term *vimâna* applied to later Dravidian temples, has originally the same sense of 'vehicle' or 'moving palace.' Something of the sense of life belonging to older vehicles remains associated with later buildings." [8]

The temple car is a vestige of the past. It represents the temple of an earlier day when the chief building material was wood. In South India, as in other parts of the country, wooden architecture preceded stone architecture. Although the people learnt to build their temples with more durable material like stone, they retained the older form of the temple on account of their conservative temperament.

References :—

[1] Longhurst ... Report of Arch. Dept., Southern Circle, 1915-16, p. 35.
[2] Do. ... Ibid.
[3] Jouveau Dubreuil. Conjeeveram Inscription of Mahêndra I.
[4] Do. ... Ibid.
[5] Longhurst ... Memoirs of the Archaeological Survey, No. 17. The Pallava Architecture, Part I, pp. 22-3.
[6] Gopinātha Rao ... Epigraphia Indica, Vol. XV, p. 15.
[7] Rām Rāz ... Essay on the Indian Architecture, pp. 48-49.
[8] A. K. Kumāraswāmy. Arts & Crafts, pp. 118-119.

CHAPTER XIII

THE DOLMEN TEMPLE AND THE TODA BOATH

We have yet to determine the way in which the early South Indian temple acquired the *vimâna*. The current theory about it has already been stated in a previous chapter, where we expressed our disagreement with it. It is not true that the South Indian temple builders borrowed the Buddhist *stûpa* and placed it as an ornament over the sanctum. There are certain facts which go against this theory.

In the course of our preceding discussion, we have noted two types of South Indian temples: (1) the dolmen temple, and (2) the Toda 'boath.' It is with the latter that we are concerned at present, for its presence removes the necessity of borrowing the *vimâna* from the Buddhists. The 'boath' appears to represent the prototype of the South Indian *vimâna* which seems to be as much indigenous to the soil of the South as the temple itself.

The Toda 'boath' has already been described in a different context, when we noted its resemblance to the shrines of Vetâḷa. It is necessary that we should know something more about it. We have to determine whether it is Indo-Aryan or Dravidian in its origin. The problem is really difficult. The Toda 'boath' shows a striking resemblance to the Âryâvarta temple. A comparison of the Bodh-Gaya plaque, and the 'boath' brings out all points of resemblance very clearly. The conical tower, the *sikhara*, and the arched gateway have their counterparts in the conical hut-shrine, the stone placed on the top, and the low arched-doorway. There is, however, one point of difference. Although the *prâkâra* round the shrine in the Bodh-Gaya plaque corresponds to the rude wall of uncemented stones round the 'boath', the former is rectangular in form, whereas the latter is circular. Nevertheless the resemblance is remarkable. It is due to the fact that the temple of the Bodh-Gaya plaque and other Âryâvarta temples were originally modelled upon a hut-shrine similar to the Toda 'boath.' It may also be interesting to note that the Todas are semi-pastoral people, and that they have not

The Boath.

Taken from the *Madras Journal of Literature and Science.*

yet completely shaken off their nomadic habits. They are accustomed to migrate during certain seasons of the year with their cattle and their gods.

However, the 'boath' shows at the same time certain very strong Dravidian affinities. Its resemblance to the Vetāḷa shrines is noted on more than one occasion. The Pêy temples of the Tinnevelly district are also said to be similar in form. The resemblance between the Toda 'boath' and the Pêy temple has so struck the attention of Gustav Oppert that he remarks as follows: "These obelisk shrines represent a very ancient style of architecture. It is bere worth mentioning that of the two kinds of temples which are found among the Todas, the boa (boath) which is regarded as the older form of building and of which there are only three or four left on the hills, *is such a conical structure* looking from a distance exactly like a church-steeple."[1]

We consider, therefore, that the Toda 'boath' represents the most primitive Dravidian architectural style. Its resemblance to the Âryâvarta temple can be satisfactorily accounted for by assuming that the Âryans borrowed this type of temple from the Dravidians, during the early days of their migration into India. It became in course of time the only type of temple known in the North, whereas it was profoundly affected by the dolmen temple which had grown up later in the South. These two types of primitive temples must have been existing side by side at one time in South India. With the expansion of the Âryans to the south, a change came over these temples. The contact between the two peoples resulted in the complete aryanisation not only of the Dravidian culture but of their religion. The Dravidian deities were admitted into the pantheon of Âryan gods, the males being recognised as the sons or the aspects, and the females as the wives of the new divinities. The Dravidian and the Âryan gods became members of one divine community and had to live together.

This religious syncretism produced a similar syncretism in the temple. When a Dravidian goddess married an Âryan god, they came to live together in a common dwelling place; but each of them had his or her own house before their marriage. Neither was willing to give up his or her abode in favour of the other.* A compromise was necessary. Such a compromise was made possible by the presence of the boa-type shrine which appeared as an exact counterpart of the Âryan temple. It must be remembered in this connection that the temples of Âryan gods had their origin in a primitive Dravidian hut-shrine, resembling the 'boa.' The boa-shrine was, therefore, superimposed upon the dolmen temple, and this resulted in the birth of the pre-Pallava temple of South India. The newly married couple lived happily under this new roof. The temple that was thus evolved was further subjected to Buddhistic influences and culminated in the production of the style of architecture which we see at Mahâbalipuram.

Thus it was that the modern Dravidian temple grew up. Every part of the temple has its own significance, and no part is added for the sake of mere ornamentation. The *vimāna* is as necessary a part of our temple as the sanctum itself. That is why our *śilpis* say that a temple without a *vimāna* is like a man without a head.[3] However, further consideration of this important and intricate subject will be left over for another occasion.

This syncretism of the Âryan and the Dravidian religions is aptly illustrated by the history of Śaivism. Śiva or Rudra is the typical Âryan conquering god, who advanced towards the south, conquering and absorbing the religions of the original inhabitants of the south. That is why Śaivism still remains, in one form or another the national religion of South India. We shall, at present, do no more than to barely illustrate what we have said by means of a few select legends associated with some important gods.†

Seven kings who were 'reigning in a certain city' neglected to worship the Śakti (the local presiding deity) of the place. At first taking the form of an Erukala (gipsy) woman, she went to the eldest of the kings to persuade him to show her proper respect. But he drove her away. Next, disguising herself as a monk, a follower of Śiva of whom, by the way, the king was

* This is still seen in the temples dedicated to Śiva. The god lives in one shrine, and the goddess in another. There are two separate temples, although they are situated in the same compound.

† The subject will be dealt with more adequately in my essay upon the Origins of the Linga Cult.

a worshipper, she approached the king, and requested him to give her 'a rock in a desert place.' On securing what she desired, she ploughed the ground and planted a garden. She brought some flowers from this garden to the king, and told him that 'Śiva would be much pleased if he (the king) would use them in daily worship.' The king then appointed her to supply him with flowers regularly for his daily worship. At last she induced him to go to the garden, and himself pluck the flowers, urging that by this act he would please Śiva more. One day, while he was in the garden gathering flowers as usual, the Śakti took him unawares and had him surrounded by her attendants. Then she appeared before him in her real form, and told him that unless he instituted her worship, she would have him impaled. The king refused to yield to her, and he was impaled. The place where he was impaled came to be known as Korlapâḍu, and the goddess Korlapâṭi Ankamma.[3]

Here is the story of king Rudra. He was the last son of a Brahman named Vīra Kalita Râja. The latter was a great *bhakta* of Pôlêramma. While still in the womb of his mother, Rudra had taken a vow not to worship the favourite deity of his father. Some years after his birth, he was elected king of his place. Thereupon he prohibited the worship of Pôlêramma, and even desecrated her temple. The goddess became indignant and resolved to take vengeance upon the king. With the aid of Mâtamma and her brother Pôta-Râzu, she created 'three hundred and sixty diseases' which she spread in the community. The king himself was stricken with disease 'and was at the point of death.' He would not consent to worship Pôlêramma even then. But the mother of the king went to the goddess in secret, and implored her to spare the life of her royal son. The goddess demanded impossible conditions. The king was informed of this; but he did not accede to them. Then a *jâtara* was declared by Pôta-Râzu. Diseases increased in the place. Men and cattle began to die in hundreds. Mâtamma announced in the town that all the misfortunes of the people had their origin in the king's refusal to worship Pôlêramma. 'King Rudra hearing this, consented with all his people to worship Ammavâru . . . .'[4]

The story of the marriage of Mīnâkshi with Śiva illustrates one stage of the fusion between the Âryan and the Dravidian religions. Mînâkshi, the goddess of Madura, married Chokkalingam, a local demon identified with Śiva.

According to the legend recorded in the *Madurai-sthala-purāṇa*, Mînâkshi succeeded her father on the throne of Madura. When she attained maturity, she was asked to choose a husband. She said that she would wage war upon the neighbouring kings, and would take as husband whosoever should vanquish her. She conquered all earthly kings, and proceeded to Kailâsa to conquer Śiva. When, however, she met the god, she found by means of a sign that he was her husband. 'The god (Śiva) asked her to return to Madura where she dwelt.' Accordingly she returned home. The preparations for the marriage were made, and all the gods were invited to attend the wedding. Then Śiva came at the appointed time, and Mînâkshi was seated by his side 'on the marriage throne, when Vishṇu joined their hands.' [5]

The Âdi-Śakti was in the beginning; once she fell in love with Vishṇu. When she proposed to Vishṇu to marry her, he asked her to give him her discus and the third eye. She gave them to him; consequently she lost half of her power. Then Vishṇu asked her to take a bath in the sea and return to him to become his spouse. Meanwhile, he drank all the water in the seas, and no water was to be had for her to bathe in. She became exceedingly angry. This frightened Brahmā, Vishṇu and Śiva. It was then that they created Viśvakarma and asked him to make them a chariot at once. When the chariot was ready, they got into it and ascended into the sky.

After much wandering, the Âdi-Śakti discovered a small pool of water in which she bathed, and returned to the place where she had left her intended spouse; but he was nowhere to be found. She began to weep bitterly, because he had deceived her. Suddenly the three gods appeared in their chariot in the skies. She begged them to take her also into their chariot. Vishṇu said that she might go up to them. She did so; but in the attempt she lost all her power, and was in a helpless condition. He then threw at her his discus and cut her into three pieces of which he took the head, Brahmā the trunk, and Śiva the legs. These three parts became three different Śaktis, Lakshmī, Sarasvatī and Pârvatī, whom the three gods married respectively. [6]

The four legends that have been cited above illustrate the various stages in the union of the Dravidian and the Âryan religions. The first legend shows the conflict between the Dravidian and the Âryan gods, and the complete defeat and destruction of the latter by the former. The second represents the conflict between the two sets of gods in which the Âryans could not be destroyed, but could only be forced to acknowledge the superiority of the Dravidians. In the third, the conflict is equal, and ends in a diplomatic marriage. The last describes the complete victory of the Âryan gods over the Dravidian. The conflict is now ended. The process of the aryanisation of the Dravidian religion is complete. Besides, traces of this syncretism can still be detected in the temple itself. In every temple tower 'there is what is called a *mukhabhadra* or front tabernacle,'[7] at the top of the tower. A stucco image of the deity within the sanctum, or of one of his avatars is invariably placed in it. Thus in the same temple, we have the principal deity in two places, one above and another below. This minor architectural detail shows that our present *vimāna* was originally an independent shrine by itself, before it was tacked on to the sanctum, the dolmen temple. The new edifice that came into being in this manner represented the pre-Pallava South Indian temple. This was later subjected to the influence of the Buddhists who left their mark on it. The monolithic temples at Mahâbalipuram exhibit the standard form of the South Indian temple, after it came under the influence of the Buddhists.

References :—

[1] Gustav Oppert ... The Original Inhabitants of India, p. 578.
[2] Ananthālwar ... Indian Architecture, Vol. I, p. 239.
[3] Elmore ... The Dravidian Gods in Hindu Religion.
[4] Do. ... Ibid.
[5] Do. ... Ibid.
[6] Do. ... Ibid.
[7] Ananthālwar ... Indian Architecture, Vol. I, p. 233.

CHAPTER XIV

THE VIMANAS OF DIFFERENT TYPES

There is another type of architecture that seems to have been known in South India in early times. The most primitive representative of this type is the Suḍalai-Mâḍan's pillar, which is a common feature of the country surrounding the town of Tinnevelly. The pillar is generally pyramidal in shape, although the conical variety is not unknown. Occasionally, pillars resembling miniature temple *vimānas* (as for instance, at Pālamcōṭṭah) are also seen. Three of these pillars generally stand together, although single ones are met with, standing here and there. They are built of bricks and mortar, but more frequently of clay. They are supposed to be the dwelling places of Suḍalai-Mâḍan or 'the lord of the cremation ground'. This appellation is fully explained by the legends associated with him. He was originally a demon of the graveyard feeding on corpses, although at present he is identified with god Śiva.

Again, we see the same style of architecture in a more developed form in another part of South India. At Mudubidri in South Canara are seen tombs of the priests. "They vary much in size and magnificence, some being from three to five or seven storeys in height." [1] In spite of what Fergusson says to the contrary, their kinship to our temple towers or *vimânas* is unmistakable. These tombs mark a stage in the development of Suḍalai's pillars. Both of them are pyramidal in shape; the tombs have storeys, whereas Suḍalai's pillars have generally none.

The next stage in the growth of this type of building is generally seen in our graveyards. Over a good number of graves are found structures of brick and chunam which consist of a series of square platforms placed one above the other. The platform at the bottom is the biggest in the series. The one above it is smaller than that in size; the next still smaller, and so on. The whole structure, if of sufficient height, resembles a temple tower in miniature. Sometimes this structure is built on a basement of solid brick. Then its resemblance to a temple is complete.

The Graves of the Priests at Mudbidri.

Taken from Fergusson's *Indian and Eastern Architecture*.

Sou ndian Hindı 'ave

Set Mehal Prasada

Taken from Fergusson's *Indian and Eastern Architecture.*

For the next stage of development, we have to cross the narrow Gulf of Mannar and go to Ceylon. At Pollonnaruva in Ceylon, there stands a building called the 'Set Mehal Prasada.' According to Fergusson, "it is one of the most perfect representations existing of the seven-storeyed temples of Assyria."[2] Its kinship with the *rathas* of Mahâbalipura and other buildings of the Dravidian style is admitted on all hands.

These structures are closely related to one another. In fact, they belong to the same style of architecture. This also is shown by their association with the graveyard. The connection of the first three with the cemetery is already noted: that the last one also is similarly related to it is seen by the close association of the 'Seth Mehal Prasad' with a splendid dolmen which stands before it. Thus, there is an inner unity binding them all together into a single class. To the same class belongs the temple with the pyramidal *vimâna* and the dome-shaped *sikhara*. Havell calls this *sikhara* Siva's dome. If he is right in this, the connection of this kind of *vimâna* with the above is at once established. It is a well-known fact that some of our important Śiva shrines are actually built upon graves. In some of the important places of pilgrimage, the temple of Śiva stands or had at one time stood on the cremation ground. In this connection, it may be interesting to note that Suḍalai whose temple we have already described is identified with Śiva. There appears to be some justification for this identification; for Suḍalai, the lord of the cremation ground, cannot after all be very different from Rudra, the lord of the *rudra-bhûmi* or 'the crematorium.'

The above considerations seem to justify us in concluding that the pyramidal *vimâna* marks the final stage of development of the primitive type of Dravidian architecture represented by Suḍalai-Mâḍan's pillars.

Another variety of the above type is the *vimâna* with the barrel-shaped summit. The *sikhara* of this kind of *vimâna* bears a striking resemblance to the roof of the Buddhist *chaitya*. A comparative study of the *vimâna* of the Śrî-Ranganâtha temple at Srîrangam or of some of the *rathas* at Mahâbalipuram, and the structural *chaitya* at once reveals their kinship. It is generally inferred from this that the *vimâna* with the barrel-shaped summit is derived from the Buddhist *chaitya*. It may be admitted that some of the *vimânas* belonging to this class are modelled upon Buddhist *chaityas*; but that does not mean that the one is derived from the other. The style of architecture seen in the *chaitya* is very primitive and pre-Buddhistic. This has already been noted by Fergusson. According to him, "the external forms or construction of these halls" bear very close resemblance to "the huts of the Todas on the Nilagiri Hills." He says, "Their roofs have precisely the same elliptical forms as the *chaitya* with the ridge, giving the ogee form externally, and altogether, whether by accident or by design, they are miniature *chaitya* halls." He adds further, "Such forms may have existed in India two thousand years ago, and may have given rise to the peculiarities of the *chaitya* halls, but it is, of course, impossible to prove it."[3]

We have shown in a previous context that the *chaitya* was not invented by the Buddhists. It was in existence much earlier than the time of the Buddha and was commonly venerated by all the Hindus. It was still an important Hindu institution at the time of Kauṭilya. Moreover, it is clear from the *Arthaśâstra* that the *chaitya* was a structural building. Its external appearance could not have been very different from that of the shrine found among the bas-reliefs of Barhut which in the language of Fergusson is "so exactly like the ratha here (at Mahavellipore), that there can be no doubt that such buildings were used in the North of India two centuries at least before Christ."[4] It is not unreasonable to conclude from this that the *rathas* at Mahâbalipura and consequently the *vimânas* with the barrel-shaped summits are the lineal descendants of the pre-Buddhiṣtic Hindu *chaitya*. Perhaps, the modern Tamil temple of Ceylon which Fergusson mentions (Bk. IV, ch. II) may be taken as a fair representation of the intermediate stage in the development of the primitive *chaitya* into our modern temple *vimâna*.*

* The resemblance which the Toda hut bears to the external appearance of the *chaitya* is noticed above. It is also pointed out that it is pre-Buddhistic in origin. There are two points which we must keep in mind in connection with the primitive chaitya: its early association with graves, and its later use as shrine. We must see whether there is anything corresponding to these two in the Toda hut. Every Toda settlement has a dairy attached to it. In a Toda village the dairy takes the place of a temple. Two or three priests attend to the work of the dairy, and look after the sacred herd of buffaloes belonging to it. The dairy or

A Ratha at Mahabalipura.

Taken from Havell's *Indian Architecture.*

A Hindu Temple in Ceylon

From Fergusson's *Indian and Eastern Architecture.*

the *teriari* as it is called, is an ordinary Toda hut, specially intended for the purposes of religion. Moreover, it is also used as a death chamber on occasions; when a male member of a settlement dies, the corpse is removed to the dairy where it is kept until it is carried to the cremation ground. When, however, a woman dies, a separate hut of the ordinary type is specially built to keep her corpse in. These points bring out clearly the resemblance between the chaitya and Toda dairy.

Moreover, the Toda dairy-temple appears to be directly connected with the modern Hindu temple. Every Hindu temple has a reservoir of water attached to it. It is generally called *kônêru*; and the gods are taken here sometimes for bathing. Corresponding to the *kônêru* of the Hindu temple, we have a *kwôinir* attached to every Toda dairy. "At Modr, where there was a *kwóinir* for each Palol, it was a spring built in with stones, and not a stream as at other villages." (Rivers: *Todas*, p. 85). The *kwôinir* thus brings the Toda dairy and the Hindu temple nearer.

References:—

[1] Fergusson ... Hist. of Ind. and Eastn. Architecture, p. 275.
[2] Do. ... Ibid., p. 202.
[3] Do. ... Ibid., p. 105-6.
[4] Do. ... Ibid., p. 105-6.

CHAPTER XV

THE CONCLUSION

The evolution of the South Indian temple which is the subject of the foregoing study is a complicated process; and a discussion of the subject must necessarily be complex. The facts that have been considered in the course of the investigation seem to indicate that the temple is the result of a long process of development which spreads over several centuries. The temple, which is invariably associated with gods, had, at one time, no connection with them. The gods were worshipped in the form of trees. This was the most primitive form of worship known to the original inhabitants of the land. The temple had its origin elsewhere. It originated in certain religious practices connected with the worship of the spirits of the dead, which were supposed to cause famines, epidemics and other calamities. The primitive people dreaded them much. They believed that these ghosts were unhappy and troubled men, unless they were properly treated by them. It was, therefore, considered necessary to propitiate them by offering them gifts. Moreover, the fear induced the men to take precautionary measures to protect themselves from the attacks of these spirits. An important step they adopted was to circumscribe the sphere of the malignant activity of the spirits in a magic circle of stones built around the graves where they were generally believed to hover. This led to the formation of a new cult, the most prominent feature of which was the worship of graves and tombs surrounded by stone-circles. These became the nuclei around which grew up temples in course of time.

Although the custom of erecting stone-circles around graves has long ago disappeared, vestiges of the practice still remain in secluded corners of the country which are not very much in touch with the civilized world. In some communities, such as the Todas, the stone-circle is still associated with funeral rites. The Kurumbas and the Iruḷas, however, use it not so much as a restraining circle around the grave, but as a shrine where the spirits of the dead are worshipped. The original magic circle of stones is seen here in a stage of transition, when it is being transformed into a temple. Another change also must be noticed. The place of the simple grave surrounded by a stone-circle is taken by the cairns, the cromlechs, and the dolmens. They appear to have had their origin in the primitive habit of burying a dead person in the hut in which he dies and of its subsequent abandonment. New religious ideas and perhaps new conceptions regarding the life after death, appear to have given a permanent and imperishable form to the huts which were originally built of perishable material.

Graves thus became shrines where the spirits of the dead might be worshipped. It is at this stage that these shrines began to lose their distinctive character. Their connection with the dead became dim and remote. The change was gradual and imperceptible. It was brought about by the close association of the spirits of the dead with the village deities. The temples which were originally built for the former became the places of habitation of the latter. The union of the two classes of spirits was the result of a desire for rural economy on the part of the primitive people. In order to avoid a double expenditure of money, they celebrated the anniversary of the dead of the community and the annual festival of the village deities together. The two classes of spirits which were worshipped together, could not be kept separate. In course of time, they naturally fell together and formed a single community of spirits. This resulted in the emergence of a new cult which retained some features of both the older cults. The village deities who had originally no temples, acquired them by association with the spirits of the dead.

The original religion of the Dravidians consisted of the worship of ancestral spirits and village gods. It was considerably modified by the contact of the Dravidians with the Âryans. As a result of Âryan invasions of South India, the Dravidian religion was completely aryanised. The gods of the two races united together and formed a single hierarchy. The temples which were connected with the primitive Dravidian religion became the centres of the reformed religion. The Âryan gods became thenceforward the principal residents of the Dravidian temples.

The temple which grew around the graves is the dolmen-temple. It was a building consisting of a rectangular chamber with a terraced roof. In front of this chamber, there was a hall. There was no superstructure over the roof. It was this temple which the Âryan gods acquired for themselves, when they first entered South India. It differed in certain important respects from the modern South Indian temple. The modern temple consists of a sanctum, an adjoining hall in front, and a conical or pyramidal tower called *vimâna* or *stûpi* which stands upon the sanctum. It is not easy to discover the origin of the *vimâna*. People generally believe that this feature of our temple architecture was borrowed from the Buddhistic *stûpa*; but this view is not based upon evidence. The Âryans entered South India long before the time of the Buddha. They seem to have been familiar with temples at least as early as the time of the Buddha, if not earlier. If we suppose that the Dravidians learnt the art of constructing *vimânas* from the Âryans who came to the South much earlier than the time of the Buddha, there is no need for us to think that the Dravidians borrowed the idea of *vimâna* from the proselytizing Buddhists. From very early times, there existed in South India two important types of temple, the dolmen-shaped and the hut-shaped. What really happened was that these two types coalesced under the influence of the Âryans. All the local cults of South India were united and built into a single universal cult. The result of this union was the formation of a federation of all the religious sects of South India. It was considered necessary to make concessions to the conservative ideas of the people who clung fast to some of their ancient institutions, the most important of which was their temple. The newcomers were also very unwilling to give up the temple, which was considered an integral part of their religion. Thus were brought together three kinds of temples (1) the dolmen-shaped, (2) the hut-shaped, and (3) the northern temple. The two latter types were similar in form. The so-called Aryan temple was an institution borrowed by the Âryans from the Dravidian inhabitants of Northern India in former times. This accounts for the remarkable resemblance which the hut-shaped temple bears to the Āryan temple. The problem was, therefore, solved by combining the two ancient types of Dravidian temple, and evolving from it a new type which retained the most essential features of the older types. The hut-shaped temple was superimposed upon the dolmen-shaped and the result is the modern South Indian temple. It must be remembered that the amalgamation of the two ancient types would not have taken place but for the presence of the Âryan element in the reformed Dravidian religion. The modern South Indian temple is thus seen to be the result of a long process of evolution.

A careful examination of all the *vimânas* in South India reveals the existence of three varieties of which the hut-shaped *vimâna*, just considered, is one. The two others are pyramidal-shaped; but they differ from each other with regard to their summits. One of them has a dome-shaped summit, whereas the summit of the other has the form of a barrel. These varieties of *vimânas* have attracted attention long ago, and the authorities on the subject are inclined to trace their origin to foreign sources. It must be pointed out that the archtypes of these two forms are found in South India, in the Suḍalai-Mâḍan shrine and the dairy of the Todas. There is, therefore, no need for supposing that they had been borrowed from outside. We now close our study with the conclusion that every part of our temple had an indigenous origin, and a careful perusal of history tells us how the unification of its various parts into a single whole has been brought about.

INDEX

PAGE

S

PAGE

W

Y